First Grade
Photographs

A Thoughtful and Practical Guide for Managing and Teaching
Literacy in the First Five Weeks and Throughout the Year

Judy Lynch

■SCHOLASTIC

New York ● Toronto ● London ● Auckland ● Sydney
Mexico City ● New Delhi ● Hong Kong ● Buenos Aires

Teaching
Resources

Dedication

I dedicate this book to my teaching partner and dear friend, Carolyn Richards, and the sweetest first-grade class of my career that you shared with me this year.

To all the first-grade teachers who have taught with me and blessed me since my first year of teaching first grade in 1984, this book represents you all with love:

Betsy Stenklyft, Joanne Devine, Joyce Mucher, Michelle Reilly, Robyn Korsen, Joyce James, Mary Allison, Ann Taylor, Becky Bickford, Debbie Stogner, Julie Bills, Cheri Murphy, Adrienne Evans, Carol Davis, Grace Perrine, Judy Croce, Gina Powell, Mary Ann Blohm-Craig, Cecelia Kingsbury, Jordie Banner, Sherry Kobane, Heather Adame, Lisa Niva, Kim Poppin, Elizabeth Turk, Frances Bigler, Kate Linares, Megan Gibb, Karen Gilligan, Barbara Manwell, Joan Mayhew, Kathy Coffelt, and Carli Baumgartner, my favorite new first-grade teacher.

To Dame Marie Clay, the founder of Reading Recovery, who passed away the year this book was written. You changed the lives of first-grade teachers and students around the world with your phenomenal knowledge of how 6-year-olds learn to read and write. You changed my teaching and my life.

To Terry Cooper at Scholastic, who asked me to write this book. Thank you for having faith in me. And to my editors, Virginia Dooley and Joanna Davis-Swing, for their constant support and brilliance!

To Doug Niva, who took many of the best pictures in this book. He is not only the consummate professional photographer but is the husband of one of my favorite first-grade teaching partners. This is the third book we have done together and I thank you from the bottom of my heart.

And of course with love to my family: Mike, Michael, Shannon, and Kevin.
This book is due the same month as Shannon's wedding—how is that going to work?
(We delayed the book, of course!)

Cover design by Ka-Yeon Kim

Interior design by Grafica

Cover and interior photos by Doug Niva, Judy Lynch, and Carolyn Richards

ISBN-13: 978-0-439-02423-5

ISBN-10: 0-439-02423-4

Copyright Judy Lynch © 2009

All rights reserved. Published by Scholastic Inc.

Printed in the U.S.A.

1 2 3 4 5 6 7 8 9   40   15 14 13 12 11 10 09

Contents

Contents

Welcome to First Grade!

When I was asked to write this book by Terry Cooper at Scholastic, I had to say no; my first-grade teaching partner had moved to another state, and I knew I couldn't do it alone. But I was excited about the concept and approached my good friend and kindergarten teacher Carolyn Richards with the idea. Carolyn, a kindergarten teacher for more than 20 years, was moving to first grade in order to use her Reading Recovery training with a whole class of six-year-olds. She said, "A year in photos? Sure—as long as nobody takes MY picture!" So we began to plan and set up a first-grade classroom completely from scratch: Carolyn a "newbie" and me a first-grade veteran (please don't say "old first-grade teacher").

This book describes our experience of that year, from setting up the classroom and introducing routines to teaching literacy skills and managing all the materials—while keeping it fresh and fun all year long! Although I have done the writing, Carolyn and I collaborated on every aspect of the teaching in this book, drawing on the accumulated wisdom of every first-grade teacher with whom we have ever taught. (Please check the dedication page to see the names of the more than 30 first-grade teachers with whom I have taught since 1984.) This book reflects the collective wisdom of us all, including Kate next door, who was new to our school this year and in her second year of teaching first grade. We stole ideas from her every time we walked through her room. Lola May said it best: "Good teachers aren't born... they're made by the teacher next door" (1982).

Our year in first grade takes place at Madison Elementary School near Sacramento, California. We are a K–6 school with about 530 students. Our school is a Title 1 school with almost 80 percent of our students on free or reduced lunch. We also have a high transience rate, with about 165 students leaving our school during this year and another 175 coming in. This class in particular had ten students leave and ten more come during the school year. Before teaching in this area, I taught in an affluent area where the majority of parents had advanced degrees and the first graders went on more exotic trips than I ever did. Both groups of students need the careful differentiation you get with guided reading, writer's workshop, and a balance between whole-group and small-group lessons.

This book is intended for teachers in their first five years of teaching first grade or returning to this magical grade level. For veteran teachers, this book will give you some new twists on your tried and true ideas and validate all your best practices. It should spark discussion with your first-grade teaching team and you will surely come up with even better ideas. It is the collaboration with "the teacher next door" that counts!

Preparing Materials for Next Year

As one school year is winding down, I'm already thinking about the start of the next year coming up. Do I want to prepare materials for the start of school in August by myself or do I want to get some help now? I want to use all the help I can get now!

So I get student helpers to start making materials for the following year. I'd be in serious trouble without these fabulous intermediate students. Sometimes they are former students but I take any willing student who peeks in my door asking, "Do you need any help?" I use the ones who will stick with it and work quietly in the back of the room. This year I recruited Destiny and Vera, who are finishing fifth grade. Of course I check with their teachers to see if they can miss some class time in the afternoon. This is usually no problem, because they are winding down their year too, cleaning out desks and so forth. My priority is to have them make word wall books and reading response journals and sometimes writer's workshop journals. Stapled together with construction paper covers, these booklets will be ready when those fresh first-grade faces arrive after a too-short vacation.

The end of the school year can be a prime time for preparing for the next year in first grade—with eager workers!

Principal Jim McLaughlin records *Green Eggs and Ham* for the listening center.

"Mystery Readers" for the Listening Center

Preparing for the next year is also a time to add to our collection of "Mystery Readers" for the Listening Center. This is an inexpensive way to have recorded stories to go with books we already have. Popular people to ask to record are the principal, cook, secretary, kindergarten teachers, custodian, other first-grade teachers, parents, and your own family.

MATERIALS ("OLD SCHOOL")

◎ **Tape recorder, blank tapes, and a microphone** if you can get one
Inexpensive resource for short tapes: 10-pack of 30-minute tapes, $6.70 = $.67 each from Blank Media (**www.tape.com**)
5-pack of 10-minute blank cassettes, Item #4321, $4.50 = $.90 each from Crystal Springs Books (**www.crystalspringsbooks.com**)

◎ **Bell or chime** to signal when to turn the page and a copy of the "Taping Tips," below.

MATERIALS (NEW TECHNOLOGY)

◎ **Voice recorder with a microphone** to record the story on your computer to burn a CD or transfer to an MP3 player

◎ **CD or MP3 player** with speakers

◎ **Bell or chime** to signal when to turn the page and a copy of the "Taping Tips," below.

Tips to give volunteers making a tape for you:

TAPING TIPS

Thank you for making a recording of this book for our first-grade class to enjoy. Here are some suggestions that will help:

1. Work in a very quiet place.

2. Practice reading the story aloud several times before recording.

3. Read slowly and with great expression.

4. Enlist the help of others if you want to add other voices, animal sounds, and so on.

5. Press record, count to 4, and begin.

6. Ring the bell at the end of the right-hand page, allow time for students to turn the page too, then proceed reading on the next page.

7. When finished, tell the listeners who you are and remind them to keep it a secret for the next group.

8. Rewind and check that you are satisfied with the sound quality, pacing, and expression.

Thank you for being our newest "Mystery Reader"!

2 Setting Up the Classroom Before School Starts

I like to set up the classroom at my own pace, long before the required back-to-school days. The days right before school starts are taken up with meetings and lots of wonderful interruptions when other teachers peek in to say hello and catch up on summer news. I like to get a jump start on the year by making sure I have at least three interruption-free days to set up the classroom from scratch.

The room looks spacious . . .

Room Arrangement: Starting From Scratch

The first step is to consider the best arrangement for your first-grade classroom. So that I don't have to push heavy things around more than once, I always measure the room first. I transfer my measurements to 1/8" graph paper so that each foot = ¼". This year, I sketched

. . . until we unpack our stuff!

it out several times, wearing out at least one eraser because I kept changing my mind as I considered:

- Traffic flow, visibility, and optimal storage

- Placement of furniture around doors, windows, outlets, and computer lines

- Wall and floor space for key teaching areas: calendar with floor seating, student tables and a reading table, and literacy centers (spread out to avoid congestion)

Here's a diagram of the final arrangement.

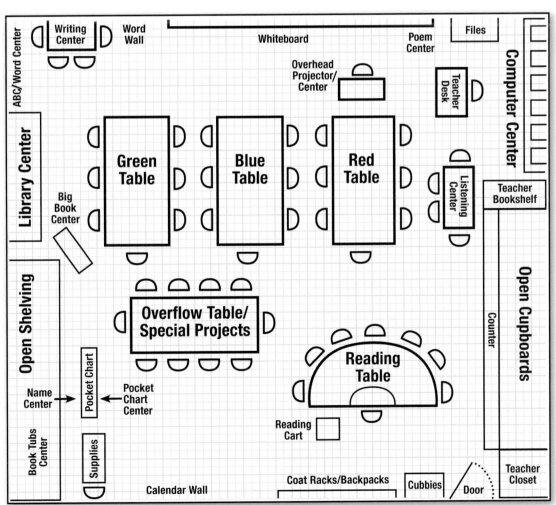

Materials to Place on Walls and Flat Surfaces

Once I've decided on the room arrangement, I consider how to store and display teaching materials such as the calendar wall, number line, ABC strip, behavior chart, word wall, student work, and so on. The photos below show how the room looks on the first day of school. I always make sure to have a graphic that helps new first graders see how they will get home. Students earn Eagle Bucks for playground rewards, and we store them in a shoe bag hung on the door.

ABC Strip and Word Wall

Eagle Buck Holder

Calendar Wall and Seating Area

How to Get Home the First Day

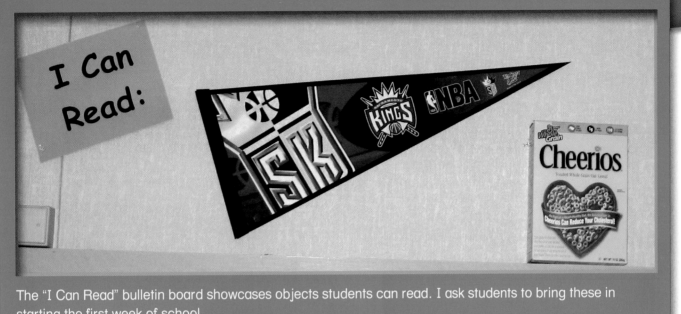

I Can Read:

The "I Can Read" bulletin board showcases objects students can read. I ask students to bring these in starting the first week of school.

On Calendar Wall

- Memory Match apple pocket chart for practicing word wall words
- Days in School with straws bundled by 1's, 10's and 100's
- Number chart 1–100
- Calendar
- Birthday chart
- Lost Tooth chart
- Special Person/Student of the Week

Placing Furniture and Materials

Basic Student Seating I decide to put the three large student tables at the front so that students can easily see the word wall, whiteboard, and screen when I use the overhead.

ON EACH STUDENT TABLE YOU WILL SEE:

- a colored plastic tray that holds crayons, scissors, and pencils for the group to share;

- a matching colored plastic tub (shoe-box size) that holds My Word books (for word wall and independent work), small journals to record center works, and writer's workshop journals; and

- charts with ABCs and high-frequency words (lists get longer as more words are learned) in vertical plastic holders.

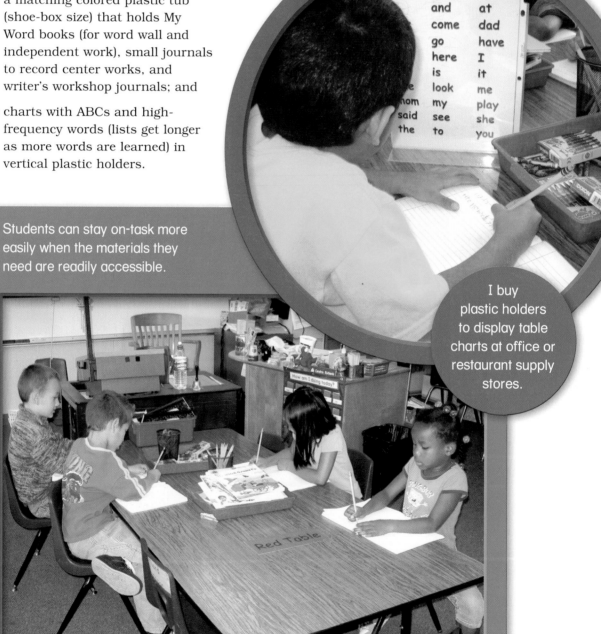

Students can stay on-task more easily when the materials they need are readily accessible.

I buy plastic holders to display table charts at office or restaurant supply stores.

I keep materials for new students in one place. I used to run around the room grabbing materials (writing/reading/center/word work journals; labels for chairs/cubbies/behavior chart; crayons, etc.) whenever a new student came. Now, I keep all the materials in one tub and a new student is welcomed and given supplies without any stress.

Five independent reading book tubs for five reading ranges are kept on low shelves for easy access during guided reading and for take-home books.

Cubbies are by the door, on an old wooden table that has drawers to hold paper for easy student access. Our pencil sharpener is also here to be near one of those rare electrical outlets.

Designing Literacy Centers

Materials for literacy centers are spread around the room to prevent congestion in any one area and are stored in a variety of ways to make the most of limited space.

2½-gallon zipper lock bags hold center materials ready to use at a table or on the rug.

◎ Hanging from coat hangers on the front whiteboard are the materials for the Poem and Reading-the-Room centers.

◎ Center materials kept on open shelves display icons that match the center chart, signaling which center they are to be used with.

◎ Some materials are housed in plastic boxes with lids that can be stacked if necessary—for example the Travel Agency and Names centers.

◎ One four-sided rack holds materials for the Pocket Chart and Names centers and the Book Tub Checkout Chart.

◎ Four book baskets reside on the shelf under the window. They hold reading response journals and books that have been read in guided reading. The book baskets are used daily for guided reading instruction, rereading familiar books from previous lessons, writing about the current book read that day, and reading with book buddies after lunch.

Open shelves

Book baskets

Travel Agency and Names centers

Planning the Schedule

First, map out the blocks of time you have the students in your classroom. My students go out for two recess periods and lunch, leaving me with four blocks of teaching time. It's not the times that matter—it's the number of blocks you have and the length of each.

7:45–9:00	1 hour 15 minute block
9:00–9:15	Morning Recess
9:15–11:00	1 hour 45 minute block
11:00–11:40	Lunch
11:40–12:50	1 hour 10 minute block
12:50–1:05	Afternoon Recess
1:05–2:15	1 hour 10 minute block

FIRST-GRADE BASIC SCHEDULE

Next, determine what you will cover during each teaching block. You'll see how I planned out my teaching time based on four blocks of more than an hour each. Please note that times within a block are always flexible.

7:45–9:00
- ★ On the rug: roll, flag, calendar math activities, shared reading with class poem and/or big book, songs, read aloud from a favorite character book (for example, Clifford) *30 minutes*
- ★ At tables: Math *45 minutes*

9:15–11:00
- ★ Guided reading groups with independent literacy centers *90 minutes*
- ★ Compu-Quick (individualized 2-minute math facts tests developed by Carolyn) *15 minutes*

11:40–12:50
- ★ Sustained reading with book buddies using "book boxes" (books read in guided reading that week and kept for familiar reading) *15 minutes*
- ★ Writer's workshop mini-lesson; writing with conferences; sharing in Author's Chair *45 minutes*
- ★ Read aloud from chapter book (for example, *Charlotte's Web*) *10 minutes*

1:05–2:15
- ★ Word wall work *10 minutes*
- ★ Memory Match *5 minutes*
- ★ Read-aloud from non-fiction thematic or seasonal books (for example, books on spiders) *10 minutes*
- ★ Monday, Tuesday, and Wednesday: Whole group basal/phonics/spelling *30 minutes*
- ★ Thursday and Friday: Thematic studies in science, health or social studies that include art and music and writing *30 minutes*
- ★ P.E. *15 minutes*

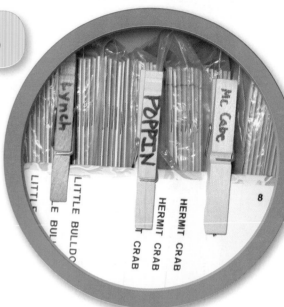

Leveling Classroom Library Books for Independent Reading

The books in our school book room are used by all K–3 teachers for guided reading.

Books are leveled according to Reading Recovery numerical levels 1–28. Some schools use the Fountas and Pinnell leveling system, in which books are labeled with letters. Excellent book lists for both are found in Schulman and Payne's book, *Guided Reading: Making It Work*, (Scholastic, 2000). Group sets of titles are borrowed and returned to the book room about every two weeks. I don't return them right after a lesson because they are important for familiar reading for the week or so; I keep them in the reading group book boxes.

Leveled books are used for guided reading, rereading practice, and writing in response to each day's story.

To complement my reading instruction, I have leveled my classroom library books into five ranges that provide for an independent reading center and a take-home book system. The tubs I use are described in the following table.

APPROXIMATE RANGE	READING RECOVERY LEVELS	FOUNTAS & PINNELL LEVELS	TYPICAL TITLES
Tub 1: Emergent	Levels 1–4	Levels A, B, C	*The Birthday Cake* by Joy Cowley *The Photo Book* by Beverly Randall
Tub 2: Early Developing	Levels 5–8	Levels D, E	*Mrs. Wishy Washy* by Joy Cowley *The Chick and the Duckling* by Mirra Ginsburg
Tub 3: Developing	Levels 9–12	Levels F, G	*Just Like Daddy* by Frank Asch *Cookie's Week* by C. Ward
Tub 4: Later Developing	Levels 13–15	Level H	*Green Eggs and Ham* by Dr. Seuss *The Great Big Enormous Turnip* by Tolstoy
Tub 5: Early Fluent	Levels 16–20	Level I, J, K	*The Very Hungry Caterpillar* by Eric Carle *Miss Nelson is Missing* by Harry Allard

Many books are now already leveled by the publishers or in book lists. But what about the books we have collected over the years? How does a first-grade teacher level them? According to Barbara Peterson in "Selecting Books for Beginning Readers" in *Bridges to Literacy* (1991), when leveling a book, we should look at what features support our readers and what challenges them. These can vary depending on the book—but trusting our teacher instinct with books will be the best way to start. If you later find a book too hard or easy for a book tub, simply change it.

Preparing Leveled Books for Checkout

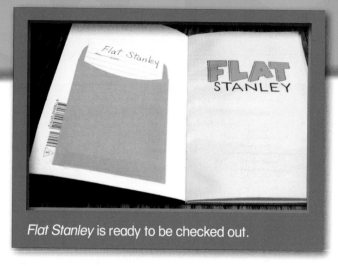

Flat Stanley is ready to be checked out.

When my intermediate-grade helpers are finished with other tasks, I put them to work on take-home books. My take-home program uses the books that are already leveled into the five ranges. As I add more books to the collection, I want them prepped to check out with the other first-grade book tubs. After I have leveled them, my young helpers put a library/book pocket (available from Resources for Reading or Demco) on the inside cover of each book. Then they make check-out cards for each one by simply writing the book title along the 3" side of a 3" x 5" index card. The card slides into the inside pocket. The checkout card will be put in a chart (see page 90) with the first grader's name on it—no sign-out needed.

These take-home books are kept in five sturdy rubber dishpan tubs that I have used over the years. For easy reading and check-out purposes, each tub has a colored dot on each side and all the books in that range have the same colored dot on the bottom left corner of the cover. These book tubs become a center for independent reading during guided reading.

Tubs of leveled books help children choose a just-right book for independent reading and take-home reading.

Pricey or Practical?
Smart Ideas for Favorite Materials

How much do we have to spend on class materials and supplies? That depends on our budget at the time. I remember one year when buying new school shoes for my own three kids trumped the fancy writer's workshop journals I wanted to buy for my incoming first graders. So I made my own, using tag covers and unlined paper from the copy room at school to get started. Most of the time over the years, I have opted for the practical, cheaper materials. I splurged this year on a large, powerful electric pencil sharpener that can sharpen different-size pencils. It sharpens a new pencil in about five seconds and can sharpen larger pencils too.

Thank goodness for my fourth-grade helper Diane, who comes in to sharpen pencils in the morning.

Center Station Storage

 PRICEY

Clear Plastic Boxes With Attached Snap Lids

14" long, 9.9" wide, 3.9" deep; $6.49 each

I bought these at my local grocery store. They are easily stacked on shelves and the lid keeps most materials contained (Names Center, Travel Agency Center, for example)

 PRACTICAL

Jumbo Zippered Plastic Bags

2.5-gallon (14 3/8" x 16"); $.31 each, $3.68 for 12

Plastic Pant/Skirt Hangers

Free

Department stores often include the hanger when you purchase pants or a skirt or will donate them happily for a school project. I was told at my favorite store that hangers "are often thrown away" and the clerk gave me ten! The best not only clip securely to hold the zippered bag full of center materials, but have a rotating hook that attaches to the white-board ledge, file cabinet handles, or other areas around the room. I tape the center icon on the front of the bag so that it matches the icon on the center chart.

PRICES All the prices listed here were current as of summer 2008. Use them to compare the pricey and practical versions of materials, but be aware that exact prices may vary.

Reading Phones

A curved tubular shape enables a student to read quietly into one end and hear clearly at the other end by their ear. The two phones made of PVC pipe listed under "Practical" can be twisted for partner reading. One student reads quietly into one end and their buddy can hear out the other.

$ PRICEY

Toobaloo

A commercial product for reading phones is offered at www.toobaloo.com and www.abcstuff.com, for $4.95 each

PRACTICAL

PVC "Phonics Phones" are offered by Crystal Springs Books, for $2.50 each

REALLY PRACTICAL

Make your own PVC phones with supplies from the plumbing section of the nearest home improvement store. Buy one 10-foot section of PVC pipe (used for sprinkler systems) that is 1 inch in diameter. Cut the pipe into 40 3-inch sections. For each phone, buy two PVC elbows that are 1 inch in diameter and twist them onto the ends of the straight 3-inch section. You have made a reading phone!

One 10-foot section of 1" PVC pipe: $3.55   (120"/3" = 40 pieces. $.09 each)

1 Ratcheting PVC Cutter = $10.79, divided by 40 pieces = $.27 each

PVC 1-inch elbows $.48 x 2 = $.96 each

Total per phone = $1.32

HINT

You may be able to get someone at the store to cut the 10-foot piece into 3-inch sections if you go on a midweek afternoon (not during spring or summer). Explain how you will use them in your classroom.

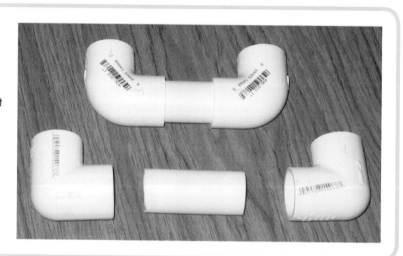

Book and Journal Holders

First-grade teachers are always looking for baskets, tubs, and crates to hold books and journals for easy access.

⑤ PRICEY

I love the sturdy, heavy, solid plastic tubs from teacher stores. They come in bright colors and will last for years. I got tired of making the practical ones below and splurged this year. The three main student tables (Red Team, Blue Team, and Green Team) each have one small shoe-box-size tub that holds their My Word Books, small journals for recording center work, and writer's workshop journals—that's a lot of journals in a small space! You can often get a 20 percent savings off these prices during back-to-school sales.

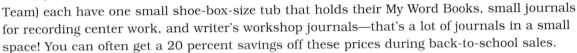

Small (shoe-box size) in red, blue, green, or yellow, $3.95 each

Large Plastic Tubs (about 9"x 12"), $6.95 each

⑥ PRACTICAL

Cover shoe boxes with contact paper for student tubs.

Contact Paper part of a roll to cover box well is about $1.50 per box

Shoe Boxes free

Student Clipboards

My students use clipboards for Writing the Room as a center during guided reading or for individual note taking on a field trip. You can find these at office supply stores.

⑤ PRICEY

Plastic Clipboards 6" x 9", $2.79 each

Hardboard 6" x 9", $1.20 each

⑥ PRACTICAL

Make your own out of cardboard and contact paper.
A roll of contact paper that is 9' x 18" can be cut into nine 1' x 18" strips. Cut cardboard from a box into 6" x 9" pieces and cover with a strip of contact paper. Add two large paper clips to secure writing paper.

Contact Paper $3.79/9 = $.42 per clipboard

Cardboard free

Pocket Chart Racks

While setting up my classroom many years ago, I noticed that two teachers from my first-grade team had metal racks to hang pocket charts or large chart paper. *Aha*, I thought, *they bought those from a fancy teacher store.* Wrong—they were garment racks from the local department store. I went right over and found them in the same section as ironing boards. I finally upgraded to the "pricey" rack below because I have four sides for materials.

Name Center has names with a picture of each first grader.

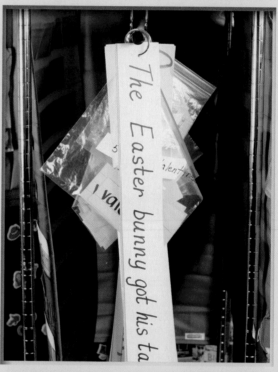

I hang "retired" poem strips and zippered bags with poem parts on key rings at one end.

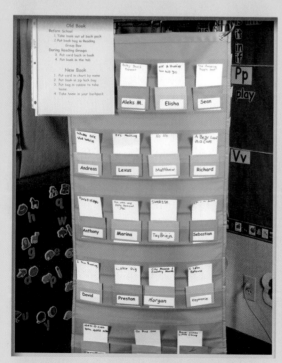

The take-home book checkout system fits on one side.

Our current poem is used daily during morning rug time.

PRICEY

Search online for "Garment Racks." I bought the "Mobile Garment Laundry Center" for $75.99, but you can find similar racks at a discount store, which is usually about $20 less. The two sides that are 36" wide can hang a pocket chart on both sides, so I have two instant centers (Pocket Chart and Names). The narrower sides are about 16" wide; one holds a slim pocket chart for take-home book checkout and the other side holds poetry strips that hang on rings. There is a sturdy rack on the top and bottom that can hold more tubs of "stuff" which we always need near the calendar or for an accessible center storage area.

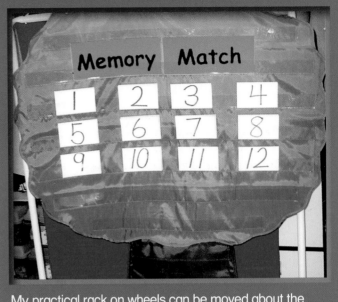

My practical rack on wheels can be moved about the room to use for centers or small-group lessons.

PRACTICAL

The cheapest garment rack from discount department stores will run about $20 but it's worth spending about $10 more to get the "Deluxe Adjustable Garment Rack." The deluxe version has a top shelf that you can hang pocket charts from on both sides with rings or clamps. These are simple to assemble and the wheels on the bottom make them easy to move around the classroom.

Magnetic Surfaces for Group Work

PRICEY

Cookie Sheets $7.00 to $12.00 at department stores

Magnetic Wall Paint $36.00 for a 32-ounce can

When setting up this new classroom, I wanted more space for magnetic word work. Individual magnetic boards are pricey if you use cookie sheets as some teachers do, at a cost of $7-$12 per student. Instead, I searched "magnetic paint" and came up with a child-safe source that is used for painting children's bedrooms. www.kling.com lists outlets such as paint stores and craft outlets that sell locally. I had a nice wall under the window I wanted to paint that needed two coats. I bought a 32-ounce can for $36.00 which was enough for two coats on 25 square feet. I left the medium gray paint as it was, but you can paint over it with regular paint in any color you want. Next time I think I'll paint the inside of the classroom door so that I have a magnetic surface there to attach notes and other items. Pricey? Yes, but I love having this large magnetic surface for the ABC and Word Work centers.

Magnetic wall paint provides a huge center area on an unused classroom wall.

Magnetic Small/Personal Whiteboard

Pricey but worth every penny is the one, small magnetic whiteboard with a wooden base that I use at the reading table. Because it sits upright, it hardly takes up any space and I can write on it with dry-erase markers or build a word quickly to make a point with magnetic letters. (See photo at right)

9" x 12" magnetic write on/wipe off lap board #MB035, $4.99

lap board stand   4" x 9" wooden base   #LH008, $4.95

Both at www.abcstuff.com

 PRACTICAL

Oil Drip Pan

A portable, inexpensive magnetic surface can be found in your local automotive store or online. I consider the 26" x 36" oil drip pan a good deal because it creates a large surface for more than one student to use. It compares to the more expensive magnetic paint for creating a surface for large magnetic work.

I found a 26" x 36" pan for $10.88 and a 17.5" x 25" pan for $8.95.

Burner Covers

Small individual stove burner covers can be found in the housewares department of local discount stores such as Target or K-Mart. You can put them to use in your classroom as personal magnetic boards. I like the white, square burner covers that originally came out about ten years ago (see photo on page 25).

You can also get a set of four white Burner Cover Magnetic Boards from Resources for Reading (1-800-ART-READ or www.abcstuff.com), Item #MB010 for about $8.29 or $2.08 each.

File Cabinets or Old Radiator Covers Free

Student Whiteboards for Individual Use

 PRICEY

Most teacher supply stores carry small whiteboards for individual students to use. I use them in literacy centers, at the reading table, or during whole-class math practice.

6" x 9", $1.25   9" x 12", $2.40   at www.abcstuff.com

In the building supply area of your local home improvement store you can find large sheets of white laminated wallboard used in shower enclosures. The price for the sheet is reasonable, but paying for it to be cut into 12" x 12" boards can get expensive. Try going when the store is not busy (midweek, early afternoon, for example) and explain what the sheet will be used for. You may find someone who will cut it for free—it doesn't hurt to ask nicely!

4' x 8' x 3/25" white tile board or melamine-finished tilepane, $12.97,

cut into 12" x 12" = 32 personal whiteboards, $.41 each

Erasers

For a quick erase of whiteboard work, small erasers are all that's needed.

💲 PRICEY

Erasers 2 ½" long, $.99 (from teacher supply or office stores)

Mini-Size Felt Erasers 2" x 1 ¼" $.50

⚙ PRACTICAL

A White Sock
each child brings from home, free

Magnetic Letters

💲 PRICEY

Talk to other teachers for the best prices in your area. My favorite source is Resources for Reading (1-800-ART-READ or www.abcstuff.com).

⚙ PRACTICAL

I love to ask for donations at the beginning of the year. Parents want to help if they can and are often eager to get the magnetic letters off the home refrigerator (Free.)

Letter Storage for Word Making

$ PRICEY

Letter Storage Boxes from teacher supply companies, $20–$30

C PRACTICAL

In the automotive section of discount department stores, look for 30-drawer plastic boxes (to hold small parts like nuts and bolts). They are small, easy to store and lightweight to carry to a table. I have one for paper letters and one for magnetic letters.

$12

C REALLY PRACTICAL

Cupcake Tins from the kitchen cupboard or zippered bags from the drawer—Cheap!

Tool kit boxes hold letters for word work.

My original letter storage—a zippered bag for each letter.

Materials I Can't Teach Without

PC Highlighters

These pliable plastic highlighters come in 24-piece sets (2 ½" x 6" each) or full sheets that can be custom fit. They come in four colors: lime green, hot pink, neon blue, and orange. The "PC" stands for Pocket Chart but I use them in a variety of ways to highlight words and word parts, as shown in the photos below.

ON THE OVERHEAD When making words with magnetic letters, we can highlight word chunks as we talk about them.

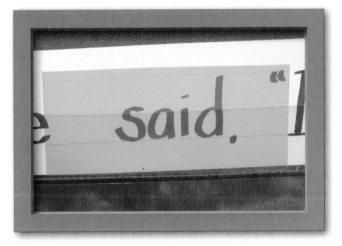

IN THE POCKET CHART As we sort words for making words or while working with poetry, students can highlight the words or word parts.

AT THE READING TABLE When making a teaching point, in a student's book or on the small whiteboard, the highlighter is very dramatic and "pops" a word or word part off the page.

WITH A BIG BOOK Before starting a new Big Book, I can have students come up and show what they know. Holding a PC highlighter, they cover up what they know and tell the group. This activity includes everyone because both known letters and whole words can be featured.

Translucent Chips

These multicolor see-through chips are ¾" in diameter. I always keep a few at the reading table. When a child hesitates on a word, I can lay the chip over just that word to highlight it or just the word part I want to draw attention to. I can also hand the chip to the first grader and have the student cover a part he or she knows—a quick way into decoding an unknown word. I also keep a few chips in my pocket when listening to students read so that this scaffold is handy.

To say I love you!

Colored chips make a word or word part "pop" off the page, drawing first graders' attention to the print.

Colored chips are also useful in writer's workshop. A child who spells *frog* as "fg" needs to say the word slowly to hear all the sounds. I can draw four Elkonin boxes to represent each sound and use four colored chips to represent each letter in *frog*. As I say the word slowly, I show the student how to push up a chip for each sound we hear. Then the students can put the letters into the boxes to match the sounds. Pushing sounds in boxes helps first graders segment sounds and then blend them into a familiar word. (Credit and thanks to Marie Clay and Reading Recovery for this strategy.)

PRACTICAL

Resources for Reading
1-800- ART-READ

Listed as "Translucent Counters," nonmagnetic,
250 chips, $3.50

One container can be shared by all first-grade teachers,
$.0125 cents each

REALLY PRACTICAL

First-grade teachers often have these chips with their math manipulatives as counters or with overhead projector materials.

Free

Letter/Word Frames

It is very inexpensive to make frames to use when listening to a child read. I keep the sizes shown below at the reading table. I also keep some in my pocket when listening to individual students read as I move about the room during sustained silent reading. The cutout middle of the colored frame focuses first graders' eyes on a word or part of a word. As they progress developmentally, I might use the open square in the middle to pay attention to

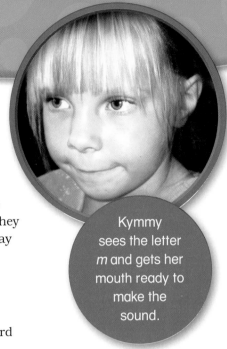

- beginning letters and sounds
- word endings and suffixes
- a part of the word that they know and can use to read the whole word
- word chunks/rime patterns that we want them to see as a whole unit
- prefixes or suffixes

PRACTICAL

You can make your own colored plastic frames in a variety of colors. You can find the materials in the back-to-school section of grocery or office supply stores. Just buy the colored see-through plastic report covers and use a utility knife to cut out the middle areas (see below). I use different-color plastics with different size openings. You can share these with other first-grade teachers at your school or share the one-time task of making them.

$1.20–$2.50 at office supply stores

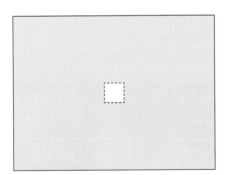
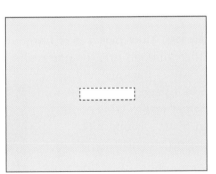
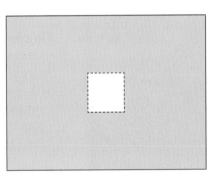

White Post-it Tape

This labeling and cover-up tape made by 3M is found at copy shops and office supply stores. With first graders I call it "boo boo tape" because it covers up mistakes we make in interactive writing on chart paper. I also use it occasionally in a student's journal when doing paired writing.

I get the 1" wide tape and keep it near the writing chart in the calendar area.
It costs about $5.00 and the 700 inches last a long time.

The reading and writing done during the first five weeks of first grade establish the materials and routines for learning the rest of the year. I purposefully choose lessons that use Big Books, poetry, students' names, high-frequency word wall words, and writing that will lead to independent work with literacy materials. The first five weeks are a training period for later work in centers, but I want the experiences to be authentic and purposeful. This is a powerful time for first graders to establish foundational skills with materials they will later use independently while I teach reading groups. Here are weekly lesson suggestions to establish this groundwork.

Trevor takes his turn as "teacher" and points under words in our I Can Read Big Book.

Shared Reading With Big Books

7–10 MINUTES IN THE MORNING

I begin the year with simple Big Books (usually 11" x 17") that I made myself. They contain repetitive patterns, common high-frequency words, and large print. These, or any simple Big Books that you have, lead to independent work in a Big Book Center. First graders have to be very familiar with a Big Book before they can read it independently in a center.

Days 1–5 Review/Teach: *I, a, the, like*

To make the Big Book: Take pictures of familiar text (stop sign, *boys* and *girls* on school bathroom door) and/or use realia (front of a milk carton, front of a cereal box, candy package, etc.). Glue each to a page and use this simple text pattern to label each page: I can read . . . (*stop, milk, boys, girls*, and so on).

Use to review skills:

◎ tracking
◎ one-to-one matching
◎ left-to-right directionality
◎ spacing of text
◎ known words (*I, can*)
◎ letter and sound recognition of initial letters.

We have been talking about spaces between words, and the class shows on their fingers how many spaces they see on the page.

Days 6–10 Sports

To make the Big Book: Use clip art to illustrate the various sports. Glue each image on a page and label each with this text pattern: I can play . . . (*baseball, football, basketball, soccer, tennis,* and so on).

I created this on the computer and then had a copy store enlarge the few pages to 11" x 17" in black and white on cardstock. This book cost less than 50 cents per page! I decorated the cover with trading cards and spiral-bound it together.

Use to review skills:

◎ tracking ◎ one-to-one matching ◎ left-to-right directionality ◎ spacing of text ◎ the difference between a word and a letter ◎ known words (*I, can, play*) ◎ letter and sound recognition of initial letters

Days 11–15 Weather

To make the Big Book: With markers, draw simple weather pictures of a sun, clouds, raindrops, and snowflakes on 11" x 17" cardstock. (You can also use clip art.) Label each page with this text pattern: It is . . . (*sunny, cloudy, rainy, snowy*).

Use to review skills:

◎ tracking ◎ one-to-one matching ◎ left-to-right directionality ◎ spacing of text ◎ the difference between a word and a letter ◎ known words (*it, is*) ◎ letter and sound recognition of initial letters

Days 16–25 2–3 Big Books of Your Choice

Use Big Books that have simple print to reinforce concepts about print, high-frequency words, and phonics with letter and sound recognition of initial letters. Some of my favorites are by Joy Cowley: *The Farm Concert, The Jigaree,* and *Mrs. Wishy-Washy.* The focus by the fourth week is on using the picture to verify the predicted word. First graders must learn to cross-check the picture with the initial letter or they will continue to just look at pictures and make up the text. The tool I teach them to use at this time is called "Get my mouth ready" (see page 58), just one of the word-solving tools I teach first graders. (This is part of the Word Solver's Tool Kit described in my book *Word Learning, Word Making, Word Sorting: 50 Lessons for Success,* 2002.)

Shared Reading With Poetry and Shared Writing

5—20 MINUTES IN THE MORNING

Shared reading with our "How Do You Do?" poem lays the groundwork for the following centers:

Pocket Chart Center Students use sentence strips to mix up or match words.

Poetry Center Students make a small version of the text to read independently.

Names Center Students sort names and practice phonics skills on names after they are introduced in Shared Reading.

Reading the Room Center Students read the print from the Shared Writing activity, which is posted around the room.

During the first five weeks, I use the poem daily to teach the following skills:

- tracking
- one-to-one matching
- spacing
- matching known words
- left-to-right directionality
- recognizing known words (*my, you, is, do*)
- initial letter and sound recognition with student names

Day 1 Whole-Group Shared Reading

I do whole-group shared reading with the poem. I read the poem aloud with much drama, and when I come to the third line (*My name is _____*), I put "Mrs. Lynch" in the blank of the poem (written on a sentence strip) and introduce myself. As I tell about my family, I model writing about them on small chart paper. I post this on the wall and tell the class that everyone will have a poster about them for the class to read later in an independent center (Reading the Room). Photographs can be added to each poster or the child can draw himself or herself at the top.

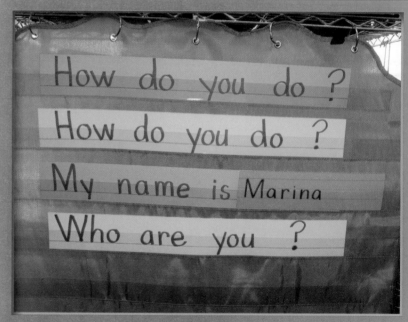

Students sort names and practice phonics skills on names after they are introduced in Shared Reading.

We play Mystery Name.

Day 2 Introduce Mystery Name

To come up with a new name each day to insert into our "How Do You Do?" poem, we play Mystery Name.

MATERIALS

◉ **Paper sleeve:** Fold one 9" x 12" sheet of colored construction paper lengthwise to 4½ by 12 inches and staple close along the 12-inch edge to create a sleeve. Draw an arrow on the back to remind yourself which way to pull out the name. (See sleeve I am holding in the photo at left.)

◉ **Name Strips:** Cut sentence strips into 9" lengths and write students' names with marker; add an accompanying photo to the right of each name.

DIRECTIONS

1. Put a different student name in the sleeve each day before students arrive.

2. Pull it out letter by letter with great fanfare. Students point to the child they think is the day's mystery name. This is great fun, especially when several students' names start with the same letter.

3. The mystery student holds his or her name card and we sing the "Vowel Song" (to the tune of "Bingo"):

> Mrs. Lynch has a student and _____ is her/his name-o,
>
> A-E-I-O-U, A-E-I-O-U, A-E-I-O-U,
>
> And _____ is her/his name-o.

Lexus points to each letter in her name as the class looks for vowels.

4. As the student points to each letter in his or her name, the class shakes their heads yes or no if the letter is or isn't a vowel. This early practice with identifying the vowels will pay dividends later when building word families with rime patterns.

5. Use the special child's name to point out any special phonics features in his or her name. The best routines for this come from Patricia Cunningham's *Phonics They Use* (1995).

6. Make a poster about each child as a Shared Writing activity. Each is posted around the room for the Reading the Room Center. (If you are short of time in the morning, this writing can be done later in the day.)

It's Aleks' turn to take home the "How Do You Do?" class book, which students practice reading with their families.

Days 2–25 Mystery Name + Shared Reading of "How Do You Do?" Poem + Shared Writing

Continue each day to reveal a new name, use that name in the shared reading of the poem, and then write about the mystery person, so that all students have a chance to tell about themselves.

How do you do?
How do you do?
My name is Korinne
Who are you?

TIP! Take a digital picture of each of your first graders on the first day of school. Insert each photo into a page for each student with his or her name in the poem. These make a great bulletin board and later a class book to send home and share with families.

Word Walls

Word Walls provide a systematic and engaging way to practice high-frequency words. Review is built into our daily routine, so students regularly chant, write, and read the words that they must know to become fluent readers.

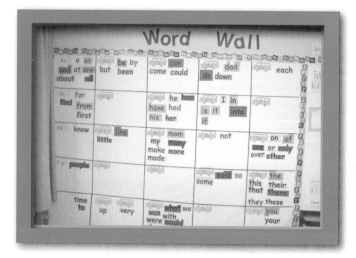

I provide students with My Word Books in which to practice writing word wall words. These books have a simple construction paper cover; the interior pages are printed on both sides with 27 blank boxes.

10–15 MINUTES A DAY LEADS TO:

◎ Memory Match (introduced week #2), a concentration-like word review game

◎ Word Center, with two center activities
   -Rainbow Writing (introduced week #3)
   -Mix-it, Fix-it (introduced week #4)

Creating the Word Wall

Before school starts, I make all the word wall words on colored cardstock, using my computer. The words are color coded so that they're in 150-point-size Comic Sans font on different-color paper within each alphabet box. This takes time only once; then the words can be saved on the computer and printed out easily each year. I cut them out and save them alphabetically in small envelopes that I keep in a plastic accordion folder. The words are ready to be put up at the rate of about five high-frequency words a week. (For word lists already made and color coded, see my book *Making Word Walls Work*, 2004.)

For the wall itself, I have had the most success with the color of the background paper offering contrast to the brightly colored words. This year I have chosen a medium blue, but white or black also gives a sharp contrast. I have quit making the word wall with a box for each letter. It is a huge waste of space to have boxes with the letters *q* and *x* by themselves. On the other hand, there are lots of "th" and "wh" words on the word wall, so I make separate boxes for them.

If I were short on space, I would put up a space-saving word wall. With a space saver, you can have 20 boxes and combine letters that have few high-frequency words (f/g, j/k, p/q/r, x/y/z).

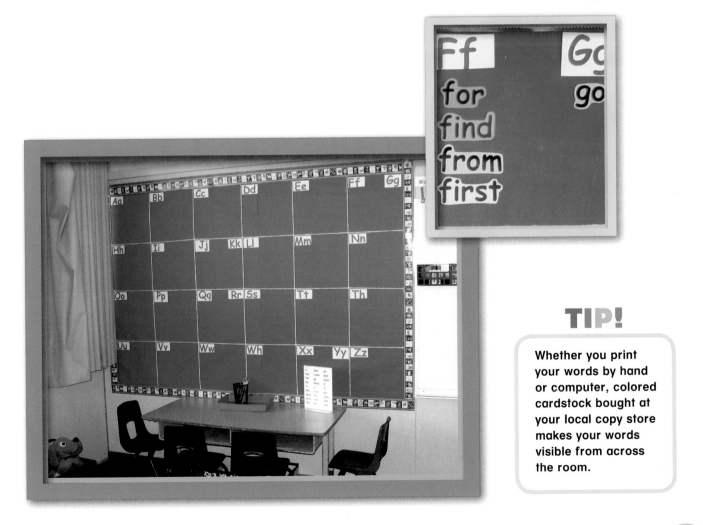

TIP!

Whether you print your words by hand or computer, colored cardstock bought at your local copy store makes your words visible from across the room.

a	and	at
are	come	dad
for	go	have
he	here	I
in	is	it
like	look	me
mom	my	play
said	see	she
the	to	you

I place charts of the 27 kindergarten sight words in upright plastic holders on all student tables and on the reading table.

Choosing Words

I like to review the words students studied in kindergarten (see photo at left). These review words are included in the 100 First-Grade Word Wall Words that I cover during the year (see below). If I have students who didn't learn these words or have forgotten them (kindergarten amnesia?), this is an opportunity to teach.

I choose words that are critical to early reading and writing. We all know that first graders start every sentence with *I*, yet on a popular 100 word list, it is number 24. I teach it first! I also make sure they can read and write *like* the first week of school or they will be writing "I lic Jessica" or "I lik football." Marie Clay, founder of Reading Recovery, called these "anchor words" because they can anchor a reader to the page. A small bank of known words helps students read the patterned text that features these words over and over.

Notice that the groups of words I teach in the first few weeks of school start with letters that do not look alike. This is intentional. It's too confusing to teach *is*, *it* and *in* together, or words that start with *b*s and *d*s, or *like* and *look*.

Aa	Bb	Cc	Dd	Ee	Ff
a are all as an at and	be because but by	came can come	dad day did do down	each eat	family friend find from first for
Gg get go good	**Hh** had here has him have his he how her	**Ii** I is if it in its	**Jj** jump	**Kk** know	**Ll** like little look love
Mm make me man mom may my	**Nn** nice no not now	**Oo** of other on out one over or	**Pp** play put	**Qq**	**Rr** read
Ss said so saw some see she	**Tt** than they that this the to them too then two	**Uu** up us	**Vv** very	**Ww** was when we who went will were what	**Xx** **Yy** you **Zz**

Sample of a completed first grade word wall (includes 20 review kindergarten words + 80 new words)

Making Word Walls Work Scholastic Teaching Resources, page 14

Charts from my book *Making Word Walls Work* (2004)

First-Grade Word Wall Words

1. a	26. friend	51. love	76. so
2. all	27. from	52. make	77. some
3. an	28. get	53. man	78. than
4. and	29. go	54. may	79. that
5. are	30. good	55. me	80. the
6. as	31. had	56. mom	81. them
7. at	32. has	57. my	82. then
8. be	33. have	58. nice	83. they
9. because	34. he	59. no	84. this
10. but	35. her	60. not	85. to
11. by	36. here	61. now	86. too
12. came	37. him	62. of	87. two
13. can	38. his	63. on	88. up
14. come	39. how	64. one	89. us
15. dad	40. I	65. or	90. very
16. day	41. if	66. other	91. was
17. did	42. in	67. out	92. we
18. do	43. is	68. over	93. went
19. down	44. it	69. play	94. were
20. each	45. its	70. put	95. what
21. eat	46. jump	71. read	96. when
22. family	47. know	72. said	97. who
23. find	48. like	73. saw	98. will
24. first	49. little	74. see	99. with
25. for	50. look	75. she	100. you

Making Word Walls Work Scholastic Teaching Resources, page 15

INTRODUCE ROUTINES

Day 1 Review/Teach: *I, a, the, like*

ROUTINES

Getting Ready

The focus the first week of first grade is on teaching the basic procedures so we can move quickly into teaching and learning for the rest of the year. I have students practice the routines and give heaps of praise until they are done right. Since I do word wall activities right after lunch, I teach students to enter the room quietly and go right to their tables. Each table team gets points on the board for doing it right. The table with the most points will get to line up first for the next recess—first graders need instant gratification and can't wait until the end of the day for a reward.

Sean is table captain and quietly passes out My Word Books.

My Word Books are made with construction paper covers. Each page is printed front and back with 27 boxes, which students like Daijah use as practice pages for writing Word Wall words.

Taking Out My Word Books

Each of the three tables has a table captain for the week. The whole class watches as I show the captain of the Red Team how to take the My Word Books from the red tub at the end of his or her table and pass them out. The only talking is a quiet thank-you when students receive their booklet. Then we watch the table captains do the same for the Blue Team and then the Green Team.

On this first day I show students where to put their name on the front of the blue cover and explain that they won't have to put it on each inside page. Because the pages are double-sided and stapled together, students can use these word books for many months for word wall work and independent work in word centers.

Introducing Words

Next, I introduce four high frequency words that are a review from kindergarten (*I*, *a*, *the*, *like*).

1. I show the colored word printed on cardstock for students to read
2. I use the overhead to show children how to write the letters in the box (our overhead transparency matches their word book)

I work at the overhead to introduce new words and model handwriting. My overhead transparency has 27 boxes to match the page the students use in their word books.

Teaching Basic Signals

Then I teach three basic signals for clapping and chanting the letters for each word.

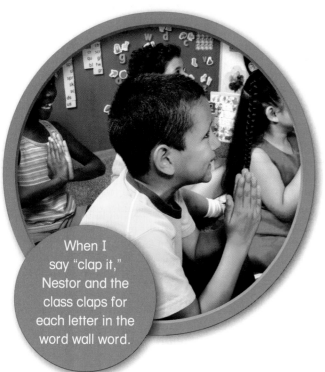

When I say "clap it," Nestor and the class claps for each letter in the word wall word.

"Ready"	Elbows to sides, hands up.
"Clap it"	Clap once for each letter while looking at the word and chanting each letter, and finish by cheering the whole word.
"Write it"	Now students can pick up their pencils and write the word in a space in their word book. I move quickly to check a few children for letter formation and then move back to the overhead to teach the next word. As soon as they are done, they must drop the pencil and assume the "Ready" position for the next word.

On the first day, I typically spend 30 minutes getting to this point. This will eventually be a 10–15 minute activity, but early on I go slow and heap praise on table groups and individuals.

Putting Books Away

I have the table captains pick up the books and put them in the colored tub at the front of the table.

INTRODUCE ROUTINES AND WORDS

Day 2 Practice Taking Out Word Wall Books

I review the procedures for passing out My Word books by the table captains and then give them the signal to begin. I count to see how long it takes to get everyone his or her book and write that number on the board as the time to beat tomorrow.

I show the class how to open the book and fold back the cover to save table space. Team points go to the first table ready. I explain that we write in the next empty box in a column and won't turn the page until all 27 word boxes are full.

Reviewing Yesterday's Words

◎ We clap for each word as it is spelled and then we all repeat the word with a cheer.

◎ I say "Write it!" and then quickly check letter formation as I move around the tables.

We are done . . . in 15 minutes!! Now we need to cement those procedures in the coming days. Eventually I would like to do this in 10 minutes.

While students write the word in their books, I check in with a few students.

Day 3 Routine Change

Putting away the My Word books is taking too long, so I introduce a new procedure. The students at tables will stay in their chairs and pass the booklets towards the end with the colored tub. Students practice handing the stack to the person next to them—with no talking and no arguing about whose book goes on top! The quietest table will line up for recess first—a popular incentive. We practice this passing of materials, a procedure good for all materials, three times. On the third time, I pretend to cover my eyes and count to five while students stay seated and pass their books to the end. I praise them for their speed and quiet teamwork. The rest of the year they are expected to have their word wall books passed to the end of the table and put away by the count of five.

Day 4 Solidify All Routines

We practice the routines from Days 1–3.

Day 5 Post the Words

With great fanfare the new words are put on the big word wall. The class tells me which letter box each word goes into and I tape them to the background paper with double stick tape. We clap and cheer for each word as it goes up.

As soon as we are done with the last word, students get ready to close their word wall books and practice passing them in.

REVIEW/TEACH ROUTINES

Days 6–10 Review/Teach: *come, go, you, is, play*

ROUTINES

"Ready" Elbows to sides, hands up.

"Write it" Students now whisper the letters as they write the words. I tell them they will remember the words better if they see it and say it and hear it.

 "Snap it" Snap fingers once for each letter while looking at the word, and chanting each letter. and finish by cheering the whole word.

 Memory Match (can be played any time you are on the rug by the calendar)

Nhu An practices snapping her fingers the first day we do "Snap It."

DIRECTIONS

◎ Using 3" x 5" cards, make two word cards for each of the previous week's words.

Example:

◎ Using a small pocket chart near the calendar area, hide the words behind index cards numbered 1–8.

◎ Ask a student to pick a number. Remove the number to reveal the word underneath. The whole class reads the word.

◎ Choose another student to call out a number. Everyone reads the second word. Do they match? If not, the numbers are returned to cover the words.

◎ Repeat until words are matched. You can spend a few minutes on this each day, but you don't have to match all the words each time you play.

(*Credit and thanks for Memory Match to Patty Calabrese*)

Words behind #1 and #8 are no match, so I will cover them again. I quickly choose another student to pick a number.

REVIEW/TEACH ROUTINES
Days 11–15 Review/Teach: *and, for, he, it, mom, see*

ROUTINES

"Ready" Elbows to sides, hands up.

"Write it" Review with students that they say the letters in a whisper as they write them and then drop their pencils to return to the ready position.

 "Slap it" Children slap their legs once for each letter while looking at the word and chanting each letter, and finish by cheering the whole word.

 Expand Memory Match Expand your pocket chart to include numbers 1–10 for words from the previous week:

 Word Practice With Rainbow Writing (later this will be in Word Center):

MATERIALS

- Word cards: 3" x 5" cards made the week before for use in Memory Match. Take one of each word card (save the duplicate of each word for next week's new center, Mix-It, Fix-It) and add them to the cumulative pile each week for practice.

- Crayons

- Students' My Word Books, or scratch paper

- A small container to hold 3" x 5" index cards

While I point to my brain, students are thinking of the word. When I point to the class, they say the word together. This gives them important "think time" and prevents just a few students blurting out the word.

All eyes are on the word as students slap their legs for each letter they chant. Learning is more permanent when we see it, say it, and feel it.

Rainbow Writing

1. Pick a word wall word and 5 crayons.
2. Write the word in 1 color, whisper the letters.
3. Repeat over the top in 4 other colors.

41

ACTIVITY DIRECTIONS (RAINBOW WRITING)

1. Pick a word wall word to copy and five crayons.

2. Write the word in one color, and whisper the letters as you write them.

3. Repeat, tracing over the top of each letter in four different colors

4. Choose another card and repeat Steps 1–3.

A laser light focuses first-grade eyes on the word *you*.

In this third week, I settle into the structure of introducing new words and reviewing all word wall words:

Monday–Wednesday From now on, these days will be spent learning the new words for the week. Cheering for each letter and writing the words continues.

Thursday–Friday From now on, these days will be spent reviewing all the words on the word wall; this weekly review helps students learn high-frequency words. Start by reading the words on the word wall—focusing on a word with a laser pointer (always kept out of reach of students). The light holds students' eyes on the word and gives them time to process it. When the light goes off, have the class say the word. Then practice chanting review words and writing them in the My Word Book that each student has ready.

WORD WALLS

WEEK 4

REVIEW ROUTINES
Days 16–20 Review/Teach:
to, in, me, at, she, have

ROUTINES

Teach mixed signals to keep students ever alert.

"Ready" Elbows to sides, hands up (we always start here).

"Clap it" Clap once for each letter while looking at the word, or

"Snap it" Snap fingers once for each letter while looking at the word, or

"Slap it" Slap hands on legs once for each letter while looking at the word.

"Write it" Pick up pencil and write the word. When done, drop the pencil and assume the "Ready" position for the next word.

When I say *Ready*, Tiana has to listen for the next prompt—Clap It, Snap It, or Slap It.

Expand Memory Match Expand your pocket chart to numbers 1–12 for review of the previous week's words:

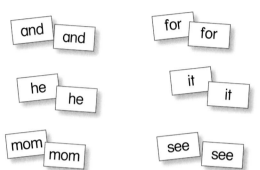

Early in the year, Ly and Nhu An work on magnetic trays on which the needed letters and word card are already placed.

Word Practice With Mix-It, Fix-It (later this will be an independent activity in Word Center):

MATERIALS

- Word Cards: 3" x 5" cards made the week before for use in Memory Match
- Magnetic letters: 2–4 of each letter arranged on side of file cabinet, oil drip pan, or any other large magnetic surface
- Container to hold cards
- My Word Books, or scratch paper
- Pencils

ACTIVITY DIRECTIONS

1. Pick a word card.
2. Make the word with magnetic letters.
3. Mix up the letters.
4. Fix the word by putting the letters in order.
5. Write the word in your My Word Wall Book.
6. Put the letters back and start over.

Later in the year, students can find the needed letters themselves and make words more independently.

REVIEW ROUTINES

Days 21–25 Review/Teach: *said, here, look, my, dad, are*

By the fifth week of school, students should be comfortable with the format of learning new words Monday through Wednesday and reviewing Word Wall words on Thursday and Friday. They should know all work-related routines:

- ◎ Getting Ready

- ◎ Taking Out My Word Books

- ◎ Putting Away My Word Books, as well as the following word-learning routines:

  - ◎ Clap It
  - ◎ Snap It
  - ◎ Memory Match
  - ◎ Mix-It Fix-It
  - ◎ Write It
  - ◎ Slap It
  - ◎ Rainbow Writing

Remember that each week's Memory Match words come from the previous week's new word wall words. All this systematic practice takes just fifteen minutes a day and leads to two word centers (Rainbow Writing and Mix-It, Fix-It) that build throughout the rest of the year.

Front-Loading Literacy Centers

The work students do during the first five weeks provides repeated practice with Big Books, the pocket chart poem, names, interactive writing, and high-frequency words in Rainbow Writing and Mix-it, Fix-it. I will introduce other simple centers in weeks 2–5.

Center Training for the First Five Weeks

LITERACY CENTERS

WEEK 1 Teaching Basic Procedures

My goal in the first week of first grade is to help students understand the general rules and procedures and to teach them how to use and clean up regular classroom materials and follow directions. During this week I focus on what I call "mini-lessons for independence." These general guidelines apply to all aspects of classroom life and will be reinforced throughout the year. I continue to teach mini-lessons for independence throughout the first five weeks; I highlight which lessons I teach each week in the following pages.

An art project the first week of school teaches procedures for using and returning classroom supplies.

Mini-Lessons for Independence: Week 1

- Listen to and follow teacher directions.
- Care for classroom materials.
- Work quietly at a table with other students.

Starting the second week of school, I begin introducing centers, one per week. I show the icon that represents the center, so students can recognize it on the task chart (see pages 49–50) and on the container that houses the center's materials. (You'll find reproducible versions of the center icons from this chapter on page 65.) With the class, I then create a chart that describes what the center will look like and sound like when students are working in it (see photo below for an example). I demonstrate particular activities in mini-lessons. I then offer opportunities for small groups to practice working in the new center under my guidance.

As each center is introduced, I show the storage place icon that matches the larger icon on our center chart. Later, this icon will also appear on our task chart.

Mini-Lessons to Introduce a Center

- Recognize center icon on the task chart and center storage area.
- Understand how to use the center's materials (where they are, how to use them, how to clean them up).
- Make and post chart that describes what center will look like and sound like.

During the first five weeks of school, I conduct the small-group center practice during the writers' workshop block. With the rest of the class engaged in independent writing, I can keep a close eye on the center work as I circulate through the classroom, helping individual writers. Once everyone in the small group masters the center by following the "What we see" and "What we hear" guidelines on the chart, the students receive "Independent Certification" for that center. Groups or individuals who don't meet the certification criteria get a chance to try again the next day.

An essential part of introducing each center is for the class to brainstorm what we will see and hear at that center. I record their notes under our chart with an eye and an ear.

ABC Center

MATERIALS

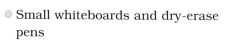

- Alphabet charts with key pictures: a-apple, b-bear ...

- Alphabet letters in uppercase and lowercase for matching and sorting (paper or magnetic)

- Pictures to match to beginning sounds (Scholastic's Little Red Tool Kit photographic magnets work well, or have students cut pictures from magazines)

- Alphabet books and very simple dictionaries

- Small whiteboards and dry-erase pens

- Optional: student journals where they can record all their center work.

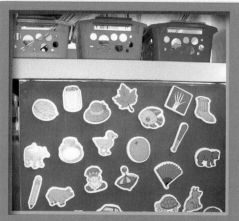

Students can practice phonemic awareness skills by sorting picture magnets by initial sound.

Specific Mini-Lessons for ABC Center

- Introduce ABC center icon.

- Make and post chart that describes what center will look like and sound like.

- Model identifying letters and writing them into a notebook.

- Brainstorm what students can do with picture magnets.

- Link phonemic awareness ("How many sounds do you hear in this word?") to phonics ("What letters should we use to match the sounds?").

- Model making a word by choosing letters that match the sounds you hear when saying the word represented by the picture magnet (see photo at left).

Mini-Lessons for Independence: Week 2

- Follow clean-up and other signals.

- Work productively.

- Be a good group member; follow the "Golden Rule."

Students can practice matching sounds to letters by stretching words and choosing letters to represent each sound. Most first graders will begin with just the initial sound but will quickly progress to hearing the ending sounds and then middle sounds.

TIP! I put out only the most basic materials to start. More materials for this and other centers can be added later once procedures are established.

Writing Center

MATERIALS

- Various sizes of paper, index cards, and envelopes
- Adding machine tape for list making
- Donated stationery and envelopes (ask a local hotel/business/print shop to donate some to your class)
- ABC and High-Frequency Words charts for reference
- Pens, pencils, date stamp
- Stapler, paper clips, tape
- Real mailbox (bought from a home improvement store)
- Tongue depressors with each student's name and cans labeled "1" and "2"
- Optional: student journals where they can record all their center work

Specific Mini-Lesson for Writing Center

Write Postcards to Friends Choose a tongue depressor from the first can to select the person who will get a card. Write that person a postcard, put it in the class mail box, and put their name in the second can.

Mini-Lessons for Independence: Week 3

- Get help and handle problems independently: "Ask three before me."
- Interrupt the teacher for a "911" emergency only.
- Know what to do when work is finished (we have students read independently until more center choices are practiced).

The flag up on the mailbox means "We've got mail!"

Each name is on a stick in the cup labeled "1." Students choose randomly from this cup so everyone gets mail.

Students must learn to work quietly in close proximity at the Writing Center.

Listening Center

MATERIALS

- Optional: student journals where they can record all their center work

- Tape recorder/CD player

- "Mystery Reader" tapes (see page 7)

- Headphones (Affix a colored dot to each pair and accompanying chair—the headphones hook over the chair back for easy storage.)

Specific Mini-Lessons for Listening Center

- How to operate the tape recorder/CD player

- How to take turns with the equipment

- How to pass out and return the books to the zippered storage bag

- How to share if there aren't enough books for everyone

Mini-Lessons for Independence: Week 4

- Store finished and unfinished work.

- Clean up a center before moving on to another.

- Match icons on centers to icons in storage areas.

Aleks can match the yellow sticky dot on his headphone to the dot on the chair back. It quickly hooks over the matching chair and prevents tangled headphone wires.

TIP! Tape over the buttons on the tape recorder that you don't want students to accidentally push.

Sometimes I have only one copy of a book and students have to learn procedures to take turns holding it for others to see.

Library Center

MATERIALS

- Stuffed animals to read with

- Book tubs grouped by first-grade favorites (Dr. Seuss, Clifford, Curious George, Frog and Toad, etc.) or topic (dinosaurs, frogs, butterflies, etc.) or a current holiday (Halloween, Valentine's Day, etc.)

- Other titles on a classroom shelf

- Optional: student journals where they can record all their center work

Specific Mini-Lessons for Library Center

- How to take a book off the shelf or out of a tub carefully and later return it

- How to "read" the pictures in the book if students can't read all the words yet

- How to record books in a journal

Mini-Lessons for Independence: Week 5

- Read the task board.

- Use task board to move from center to center.

- Center practice with the teacher watching/praising/redirecting each day.

Students will read and reread books when they have a special audience.

TIP! Label each tub with a picture for quick recognition. You can use a copy of a cover for a popular series or clip art for favorite topics or current holidays.

Looking Ahead

At the end of five weeks, students have been introduced to four centers and have achieved "independent certification" with each one. Since guided reading will begin in the sixth week, I move center time to the morning block. Now, students will do their center work when I conduct guided reading groups.

During Week 5, I introduce the task board and our rotation system. The task board uses the center icons that are displayed on the center charts and storage materials. I organize the board as shown on page 50. Each child is in a group, numbered one to four. Groups move through the centers beginning with the one listed right above their number. Once a student finishes work in that center, he or she moves to the center above it. The center icons stay the same on the board; the numbers rotate to the right so students have new starting points each day. Students do not have to go to all the centers each day—but it's clear where they are to go if they finish their work.

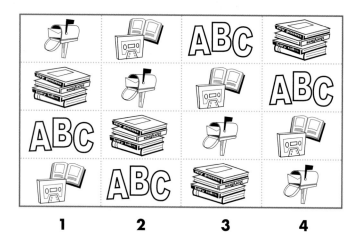

At this point in the year, first graders can function independently for extended periods of time. However, I make sure to reserve time for monitoring center work because they still require a lot of support.

I continue to add centers during the school year (see page 72–80). I introduce the centers and have students practice during our writing block. Once all students are certified in a center, I move it into the regular rotation students go through during the guided reading block.

Guided Reading: Getting Started

Basic Assessments for Grouping

In the first five weeks of school, I make sure that I have assessment information so that I can create homogeneous groups for guided reading. I do a basic assessment to gauge students' skills in phonics and word recognition, their understanding of concepts of print, and their instructional reading levels.

Phonics Test: Letter Names and Sounds

In our school district, we use The Basic Phonics Skills Test (BPST II) developed by Dr. John Shefelbine at California State University, Sacramento, as a diagnostic test in first grade. We want to check which letters and sounds our students know and which letters they confuse. It is important to note what they say when they see a letter—confusing *b/d* is common, but so is *m/n, h/n, o/c, a/d, a/c,* and even *h/y*! We can plan letter sorting activities to clear up these visual confusions in the first five weeks of school.

Angelica does a sorting of visually similar letters. This helps prevent confusing letters in reading.

Letter Sorting

When you assess first graders on letter identification, they will often name an incorrect letter. These visual confusions can be helped with sorting of magnetic letters. First graders need to look at what is unique about each letter's shape (lines, circles, curves, etc.) and where these shapes are located. The letters *b,d, p,* and *q* all have lines and circles—but in different positions. Start letter sorts with combinations of letters that do NOT look anything alike and gradually introduce more visually similar letters. As children sort the letters, they should use both hands to move quickly. Have them say the letters as they move them to the left or right of a magnetic surface (whiteboard, file cabinet etc.) Some combinations might include:

Not Alike: a/k, b/s, c/z, d/v, e/r, f/x, g/u, h/w, i/y

Somewhat Alike: c/a, f/j, m/n, o/a, i/j, w/m, u/n, w/v

Almost Alike: u/v, c/o, b/d, q/p, b/p, q/d, b/d/q, d/p/q

All of these lessons are more powerful when the child describes what is different about the letters being sorted.

Concepts of Print

Marie Clay and Reading Recovery taught us that we need to see if our first graders know how books work. Do they know the difference between a word and a letter? Can they match their finger to words read? Can they read from left to right with return sweep? Can they recognize capitals and punctuation? A quick diagnostic check on those skills will help us focus early lessons with Big Books and later in guided reading lessons.

To test concepts of print, use a simple book that has two or three lines of large print per page and a variety of punctuation marks. You'll need two 3" x 5" index cards to focus on letters and words, and a recording sheet, such as the one at left.

A quick check shows me if first graders know the difference between letters and words and other features of print.

51

High-Frequency Words

I test students on the 27 words taught in our kindergarten (see word wall section, page 34, for review lessons for these words).

Running Records

To determine students' instructional reading level, that is, books they can read with 90–94 percent accuracy, I pull a simple book with one line of repetitive text to see if they can read it. (This would be a level 1/A book.) One option is to choose a book that was introduced the day before and that they have read one time. Or I can pick an unknown book and model reading the first few patterned pages and see if they can take over the last half. Many first graders' assessments put them into early reading levels that offer support from patterned, repetitive texts.

Using Assessment Data to Group Students

Sometimes most first graders fall into the same two groups based on running records. To break these down into smaller groups and get started with guided reading in the fifth or sixth week of school, I consider other data.

Lowest Group: These students have low scores when it comes to identifying letter sounds and may not recognize all their letters because of visual confusions. Their concepts-of-print scores will be lower, and they will recognize only a few high-frequency words (often *I* and *a*).

Middle Groups: These students fall into two groups based on their knowledge of letter names and sounds and high-frequency words. The placement of students in these groups will be very fluid as I see how they progress in guided reading lessons.

Highest Group: These first graders usually know all their letter names and most sounds and are starting to use this knowledge to decode print. They have a bank of high-frequency words that they can read quickly and have mastered pointing under each word with a one-to-one match between what they see and what they say. Their running record scores show them able to read at higher levels with less support from repetitive patterns.

Checking how many words are known helps with grouping for guided reading.

Alex and Sebastian are able to work quietly in independent centers. This is essential for starting guided reading.

This is enough information to get started. Informal teacher assessment is built in every day and these groups are changed as needed. On my clipboard that keeps track of groups (see Setting Up the Reading Table, below), I write student names for each reading group in pencil—nothing is ever set in stone in first grade! I try to start with four groups but some years they spread out into five. After students have spent the first weeks of school training for independent work, I am now confident enough to start pulling reading groups. For a couple more weeks, I might only meet with two or three groups each morning to allow time to monitor center work and make sure the room is quiet and productive.

Setting Up the Reading Table

I know how important it is to have materials at my fingertips so that reading lessons go smoothly. Here's how I stock my reading table.

Small Magnetic Tray With Letters I keep a small magnetic tray (see page 24) with two copies of each letter of the alphabet. I use the letters to build key/anchor words in an emergent-level book or to show a higher-level group how to take a larger word apart in chunks.

Upright Plastic Holder I bought upright plastic holders at an office supply store. I put one at each student table, at the Writing Center, and at the reading table. To start the year, I slip in a chart of high-frequency words to review from kindergarten and our ABC Chart.

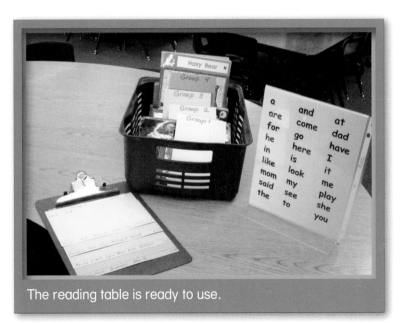

The reading table is ready to use.

Small Whiteboard I have a small whiteboard and several colors of dry-erase markers to use for teaching points. A splurge is to buy a small magnetic whiteboard that sits upright on a small wooden base (see page 23). (Because it sits up, it is a space saver and so is the small eraser.)

Clipboard I use a clipboard with 5"x 8" colored index cards to keep track of the books I use with each reading group.

I set up the clipboard with a different-color index card for each group. I tape the cards to the board in a staggered fashion so that the bottom of each card is visible. Along the bottom of each card I write the names of the children in that reading group, the current book level, and the group number (see photo at right).

On each line of the card, I write the date, that day's book title, and the writing assignment.

For example:

9-22	**Mrs. Wishy Washy**	Why was she mad at the animals?

This clipboard is useful in a variety of ways. It helps me keep track of which books I have read with each reading group. When a group comes to the reading table, they have their reading response journal open to the writing assignment from the previous day. I can check the clipboard to remind myself what I asked them to write about the day before, and then check it quickly. When it is time to take books back to the reading room, I can check the clipboard to see which books have been in group boxes the longest and have the first graders collect them.

Reading Cart

Next to the reading table I keep a small, plastic storage cart on wheels that rolls under the reading table or can sit next to the chair.

- The top shelf holds a large, rectangular basket with sets of guided reading books for the week. I use colored cardstock to section the books off by reading groups and a clipboard to keep track of each group's books.

- Three drawers hold supplies to teach guided reading:

1. The top drawer contains two small, plastic baskets. One holds dry-erase pens and small erasers that I can pull out to do a quick word-work lesson during a reading lesson. The other small basket has glue sticks that I use to do word sorts. In front is a tiny round plastic tub that holds translucent colored chips. (see page 28). I also keep pocket chart highlighters (see page 27) and letter/word frames (see page 29) in this drawer.

2. The second small drawer in the reading cart opens to hold a basket with 3" x 5" index cards, sticky notes, highlighter tape, and white removable tape I call "boo boo" tape for covering up mistakes in interactive writing. I also have some colored reusable "flags" that are sticky on one end and make good "stop signs": In longer books or chapter books, I have our reading groups put a flag or small sticky note on the last page they are to read. They make a solemn promise not to read past this "stop sign" and it helps me find the starting point quickly for the next day's lesson.

3. The bottom drawer is deeper and holds magnetic burner covers for individual word making, small whiteboards, reading phones, and a plastic cup that keeps scissors and pens upright.

Choosing Books

I take the book tub and clipboard to the book room to choose books. The book tub has colored tag dividers so that each group's books are easily placed and kept together. This is a weekly ritual. The books I choose for early lessons will typically be from levels 1 and 2.

I choose five book sets for each group so that we are set for the week. At these early levels the books are so short I typically complete a book a day with each group.

Our book room has sets of books in zippered bags arranged according to reading levels.

Early Procedures and Strategies: First Lessons Set the Stage

Passing Out Books

The first time that books are passed out, I teach the group to take their book, fold their hands and look carefully at the cover to think about the story. If I allow random page turning, the picture walk and discussion are less effective. No, Marina, Kiera, and Le'Nell are not praying in this picture, just folding their hands and following directions!

Picture Walk

Early guided reading lessons model looking at the pictures one page at a time. My questions use the vocabulary of the text and the tense of the verb. If the book says "Mom is driving," I ask, "What is mom doing in the car?" If the book says "Rain on the red car," I ask "What is the rain on here?" At this emergent reading level, students need to hear the pattern of the book while we preview the pictures.

Using High-Frequency Words as Anchors

While looking at a new book, I will point out to students that there are words they already know. Referring to our review list of words from kindergarten, I show the first graders how to frame a word by placing a pointer finger on each side. One or two known words anchor them to the repetitive text and help them notice (monitor) when it doesn't match.

1:1 Matching

I tell first graders that they must match three things:

1. Their finger

2. Their eyes

3. Their mouth

Emergent readers need to pay close attention to print, and I help them by putting on a "reading finger"—a fake fingernail available usually at Halloween. If you can't find these, a small sticker on the index finger of their dominant hand will do.

Soon students use one finger for all their pointing under words as they read. Pointing under each word crisply is an early strategy. Midway through first grade they'll no longer need their finger to point and will be using their eyes to attend to print.

"Find and frame the word *go*. That's a word you already know, isn't it?"

First graders love to point under words with a fake fingernail on their pointing finger.

Start Building a Word Solver's Tool Kit

I help students build a Word Solver's Tool Kit in first grade. Based on a developmental model of how children learn words, I start with the first thing they notice visually—the initial letter. Marie Clay reminds us that letters on a page are just a sea of print. So in early lessons I show students they need to look at the beginning of a word and tell themselves, "Get my mouth ready." When first graders look at a word, we want them to start making the sound of the first letter or letters.

Get My Mouth Ready

The phrase "Gray clouds" from Robert Kalan's book *Rain* is a great example of how students must look at the beginning letters when they read. Based on the shading color of the clouds on the page, it is hard to tell whether they are brown or gray. Children have to look at the first letters and form the sounds of the letters they see—"gr" not "br" to help them decode the word *gray*.

SCHOLASTIC TEACHING STRATEGIES • Grades K–2

Word Learning Word Making Word Sorting
50 Lessons for Success

by Judy Lynch

Ready-to-Go Lessons That Support Guided Reading, Shared Reading & Writing, and Word-Work Lessons in K–2 Classrooms

SCHOLASTIC

For specific lessons teaching the Word Solver's Tool Kit, see my book *Word Learning, Word Making, Word Sorting: 50 Lessons for Success.*

Framing the letter *m* in a book helps Marina get her mouth ready to make the sound.

Writers' Workshop: Getting Started

Writers' workshop in first grade is in the context of a complete writing program that includes all of the following:

Modeled Writing: The teacher writes on chart paper while thinking out loud about composing and correctness.

Shared Writing: The teacher writes on chart paper and first graders collaborate, sharing their ideas for composing, sounds for spelling, and suggestions for revision and editing.

Interactive: The teacher and first graders share the pen to write letters and words as we compose together on chart paper. I stress concepts about print such a words, letters, and spaces, and teach first graders to stretch a word to hear sounds in it so they can generate a phonetic spelling.

We share the pen to write our school rules interactively. Anthony concentrates as he adds the next letter we hear.

Writers' Workshop: Students' writing is the basis for group mini-lessons, individual conferences, sharing in the author's chair, and occasional publication of student books.

Writing Across the Curriculum: Students write about literature, science, and social studies topics. This can take place in a shared writing format or individual journals.

Shared writing is used to brainstorm words to describe fall leaves for a science study.

Materials for First Grade Writers' Workshop

Bound Journals

The journals can simply be paper stapled with construction paper covers (made by intermediate students or helpful parents). Bound journals can also be purchased, or if you're lucky, supplied by your school district.

Keeping students' writing organized and dated is crucial for assessing each student's growth over time. If we let individual pages go home with students each day, parents would be horrified by the early strings of letters or poor spelling in rough drafts. At back-to-school night, I explain the writing process to parents, especially how quickly phonetic spelling will improve. It is helpful to show examples of growth from a typical journal to prove our point. The parents would never have been able to tell that my former student Michael wrote "Pee wee Golf I won my papa in pee wee golf" on the first day of first grade (see right). But they can probably read a later entry he wrote: "I like to go to my grandma and my grandpa's because I love them."

"Pee wee golf I won my papa in pee wee golf"—written on the first day of school.

Date Stamp

A simple date stamp is handy until later in the year when students can write the date quickly on their own paper. In our classroom, one helper goes around the room and quietly stamps every journal. Just make sure that you're the one rotating the numbers in the date stamp each day or you'll have "unusual" dates like this one (below).

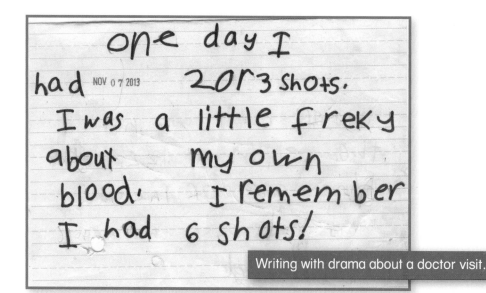

Writing with drama about a doctor visit.

Writing Conference Records

Name	Mon	Tues	Wed	Thur	Fri	Mon	Tues	Wed	Thur	Fri

C=Conference/student doing well   C=Conference   C- =Conference/concerns
☆ =Student shared in Author's Chair   P=Published   Q=Student asked a question

Teacher Clipboard

I carry a clipboard stocked with copies of my Writing Conference Records form (see sample at right). I use it to keep track of topics, conferences, skills, who has asked questions of the person in the author's chair, and who has published. I put the students' first names alphabetically down the left side of this form and run 20 copies. Each page is good for two weeks of note taking, so the clipboard is set for the school year. Without this clipboard, I easily forget who I am concerned about, who has shared in author's chair, and so on. A simple legend at the bottom enures sanity in keeping track of it all.

Writers' Workshop Basics in First Grade

- Students write daily.
- Writing craft and skills are taught in daily mini-lessons.
- Writing craft and skills are reinforced in one-to-one conferences with three to seven students each day.

5-Step Writing Process First-Grade Style

Prewrite: Teacher's mini-lessons focus on students' needs and state standards.

Draft: Most first-grade writing is in rough draft form.

Revise: Most first graders revise when they're nudged by the teacher during conferences to add to or clarify their writing.

Edit: Parent helpers or the teacher look at work for correct spelling, capitals, and punctuation before publication.

Publish: We occasionally make a book for each child. But we no longer wear ourselves out with publication. The emphasis is on time spent writing.

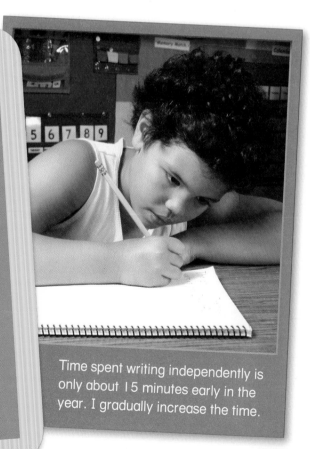

Time spent writing independently is only about 15 minutes early in the year. I gradually increase the time.

Writers' Workshop on the First Day of School

I start the first mini-lesson on the first day of school thinking aloud about being a writer. I owe my approach to Nancie Atwell and her book *In the Middle* (1998). Her method of starting a writing workshop works well with first graders too. I think aloud about three things that I might write that day. I then eliminate one because I don't know much about it. This models writing about what we know about and care about.

Thinking Like a Writer

I begin by letting students see my thought process: "We are all writers. Writers are always thinking about what they might write. Because I knew we would be writing today, I thought of writing about my son Kevin at the University at Buffalo. I have been wondering if he will keep warm this winter. I also thought about writing about watching my daughter Shannon dance last Saturday night. She was having so much fun. My other writing topic might be about our dog that died. I miss him! I guess I won't write about Kevin far away because I don't know enough details—that's a story he should write. I think I'll write about my dog. I can write about the other things another day or next week."

Brainstorming Writing Topics

I draw a circle in the middle of a poster board and write "Topics" in the center. I tell students that topics are things we enjoy writing about. I draw a line out from the center and label it "Animals." I write "Animals" instead of "Pets" because some first graders like to write about sharks and other animals that are definitely not pets. I invite the children to brainstorm other animals that they would like to write about and we add to our list. Then I ask "What can we write about besides animals?" The first child says she would like to write about her brother.

I draw another line for our web and write "Family" and we add typical family members to our list. I stop there for now on our web. We can add other topics in weeks three to five, but we already have plenty to write about for the first two weeks of school.

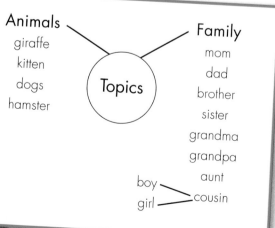

Everybody Writes!

After our brainstorming, I invite students to begin writing on a topic of their choice. I want them to have a firm idea of their writing topic, so I ask them to show thumbs up if they have a topic. I quickly call on each child to share, and I make supportive and encouraging comments: "You're going to write about your sister? What is her name? Be sure to tell us all about her and use her name." "Anacondas? Yikes, don't they squeeze you?"

Once everyone has chosen a topic, I circulate through the room, giving encouragement and asking questions to help student elaborate on their writing. "What color is your dog?" "What size do you think koalas are?" I attend to spaces and stretching sounds in words. The first one who says "How do you spell . . . ?" gets encouragement in front of the rest of the class. I ask the student to stretch the word slowly like a rubber band while looking at the ABC chart on his or her table and to put down all the letters he or she hears. I never spell for students on a rough draft or they will never apply their emerging phonetic knowledge and will always depend on me as a crutch.

When I give the stop signal, I also give them the good news: "Don't worry if you are not finished. We will write every day, and you can continue working on this same story tomorrow. Writers usually don't finish everything in one day."

Saying the word slowly and stretching sounds helps emergent writers hear and record sounds in words.

DAYS 2–25 What First-Grade Writers Need to Know

I focus the first weeks of school on some writing basics. These will be the focus of mini-lessons in writers' workshop, in conferences, and in modeled, shared, and interactive writing. Do they master these in two weeks? Of course not! We will continue to work on these for as long as needed. These are the ideas I share in mini-lessons during the first five weeks:

- What we say can be written down.

- We can practice articulating words slowly to stretch and hear sounds—"rubber band writing."

- Printed symbols are associated with sounds.

- We can record the sounds we hear in words.

- There is a one-to-one correspondence between spoken and written words (each spoken word = a written word).

- Words are made up of letters.

- Sentences are made up of words.

- We put a two-finger space between words to make them easy to read.

- Our writing moves from left to right with a return sweep—just like in books.

- We can add to the previous day's writing.

Every table has an ABC chart with pictures to help young writers match letters to the sounds they hear in a word.

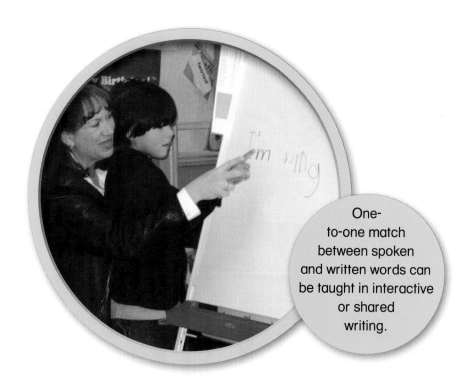

One-to-one match between spoken and written words can be taught in interactive or shared writing.

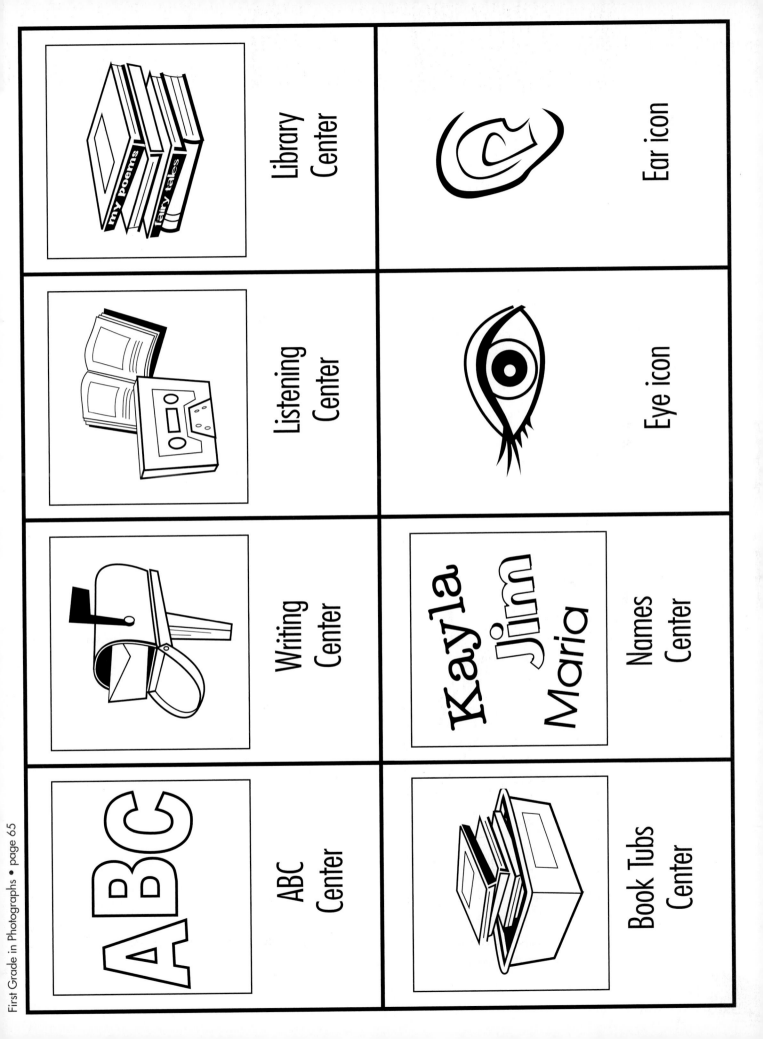

Library Center

Ear icon

Listening Center

Eye icon

Writing Center

Names Center

ABC Center

Book Tubs Center

When you ask first-grade teachers to describe their favorite part of teaching 6-year-olds, they will usually talk about the huge changes in learning they witness within a school year. As we look at literacy centers, reading instruction, and writing in this chapter, the focus will be on how we can support that steep learning curve.

Independent Routines for Literacy Center Time

After the first five weeks of school, centers are moved to the guided reading block. At this time, I introduce routines students must complete before beginning centers and after their guided reading lesson. Every day, students must:

- Read three familiar books from their reading group book box.
- Finish any writing from the yesterday's guided reading session, and
- Complete a teacher choice assignment (see page 67 for examples)

Before going to centers, every student is expected to reread three familiar books from their guided reading book box.

Nhu An chooses a new book to take home.

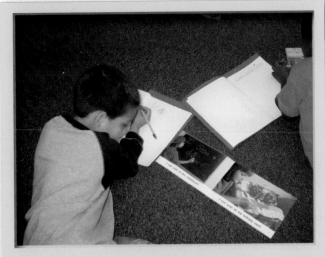

After their guided reading lessons, students reread the day's new book and write about it.

After a guided reading lesson, students must:

- Reread and write a response to the current book,
- Return their take-home book and choose a new one.

Once students have completed these routine tasks, they may begin working through the centers. I find this a win-win situation: Students are doing massive amounts of reading and writing during the guided reading block *and* they do not all rush to centers immediately. Another benefit is that with students doing so much reading and writing, I don't need as many centers!

Teacher Choice Assignments

I often assign work for the whole class to complete before they begin centers. These are just some examples of the kind of assignments I use.

- Respond to a story on which the whole class is working
- Practice spelling with Rainbow Writing
- Work in writer's workshop folder

In the spring, we read *The Doorbell Rang* by Pat Hutchins to connect literature to math. The next day, Enasia and the rest of the class were asked to write a different ending to the story as a Teacher Choice Assignment during the guided reading block. The prompt was: What would happen if Grandma did not bring more cookies and more kids rang the doorbell? Below are examples of two students' responses.

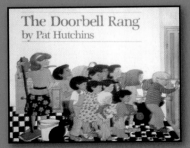

The Doorbell Rang
by Pat Hutchins

There Were 12 cookies and 12 kids, But 12 more kids came. But there Were no more Cookies so thay cut it in hafe and thay all got hafe of the cookies.

6 kids were at the door. Bell ranging and they did'int Open it.

Introducing and Maintaining Literacy Centers Throughout the Year

In the sixth week of school, I continue training for "Certification" in a few more centers during writing workshop time. The materials for the Pocket Chart, Names, and Big Books centers are very familiar to the class after we have established routines to use them independently over the first five weeks. You'll find reproducible versions of the center icons from this chapter on pages 65 and 96.

WEEK 6   Computer

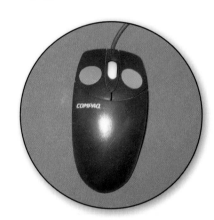

You can use the Computer Center as a listening center with books and CDs or MP3 files.

MATERIALS

- Headsets (hang on side of the monitor with a plastic self-stick hook)

- Mouse with a green dot on left side (green=go) and red dot on right side (red=stop)

- Your favorite software and Web sites (be sure to check out www.starfall.com)

Specific Mini-Lessons for the Computer Center

- Make and post a chart that describes what the center will look like and sound like.

- Use the mouse to open shortcuts, proceed through a program, and exit.

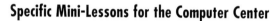

Teacher Tip

Tell parents about this Web site: www.starfall.com— named a site "too good to miss" by *The Reading Teacher* (journal of the International Reading Association). Differentiated lessons designed for first graders with full color and sound:

ABCs Letter names, sounds, with photographs, videos, and songs

Learn to Read Decodable texts to practice basic sounds, patterns, and blending

It's Fun to Read First graders choose words to insert into stories to personalize them

I'm Reading Simple-to-read plays, fiction, and non-fiction (with color photographs)

Pocket Chart

I open the Pocket Chart center with our familiar "How Do You Do?" poem (see page 32). I change the group shared poem every one to two weeks, and the old poem materials are added to the Pocket Chart Center for individual work.

MATERIALS

⊚ Large pocket chart and pocket chart rack

⊚ Poem: two copies on sentence strips (hole punch the ends, store on a ring hanging on rack)

⊚ A copy of each poem on sentence strips, cut into individual words (store in gallon-size zipped bags—bags can be hole punched and placed on ring along with sentence strips)

⊚ A few high-frequency words on sentence strips and cut into letters (store in snack-size zipped bags which can be kept inside the gallon-size bag that holds words)

⊚ Special pointers and pocket chart highlighters (see page 29)

Poetry materials hang on our four-sided rack, ready to go.

Specific Mini-Lessons for the Pocket Chart Center

⊚ Make and post a chart that describes what the center will look like and sound like.

⊚ Discuss proper and improper uses of pointers.

⊚ Review activities completed since the first week of school:

  • Point under words and read the poem.

  • Match with extra sentence strips.

  • Mix up poem's sentence strips and rebuild without a match.

⊚ Review how to take turns.

⊚ Review how to return letters to the snack-size bags and words to the gallon-size bags.

As the year progresses, so will the difficulty of the poems and the activities with each. Each activity is introduced in a mini-lesson:

  • Match cut-up words to sentence strips.

  • Rebuild with cut-up words with no sentence strips to match.

  • Rebuild high-frequency words cut into letters and match to word cards.

Andreas does word matching using our snowman poem.

Names Center

MATERIALS

◎ Name cards with and without pictures

◎ Magnetic letters to build names

◎ Pocket chart or other place to store names and materials

◎ Alphabet charts for sounds and alphabetical order

Sean and Lexus share the pointer at the Poetry center.

Specific Mini-Lessons for the Names Center

◎ Make and post a chart that describes what the center will look like and sound like.

◎ How to do name sorts and matches:

• Sort by long and short names.

• Match name cards to name cards with pictures.

• Sort by same first letter.

• Sort into alphabetical order.

• Sort by number of vowels.

• Sort by number of syllables (clap them while saying each name).

• Match first names to last.

Trevor matches names with name cards that have pictures, then records his words in his center journal.

Lexus sorts names by first letter.

WEEK 9

Big Books

MATERIALS

- Make your own Big Books for emergent first graders (see page 30).

- Buy Big Books (but be careful about choosing text that can be read independently in this center after many exposures in shared reading)

- Pointers: purchase or create your own:
  - Chopsticks with the end dipped in glue, then glitter
  - Rulers or unsharpened pencils with decorative pencil tops

Specific Mini-Lessons for the Big Book Center

- Make and post a chart that describes what the center will look like and sound like.

- How to take out and return a Big Book

- How to use pointers safely

- Taking turns and share a book

As with every new center, we brainstorm what we will see and hear at the Big Book center for a chart that will hang by the centers.

Marina, Lexus, and Kiera figured out their own way to share a popular pointer: read a page and pass the pointer.

Continuing to Add Centers as Needed

Starting in week 10, I feel comfortable adding two centers a week. The procedures for what to do at centers are well established—students are "Certified" quickly as they practice the activities and follow the expectations set out on the center chart: "What will we see?" and "What will we hear?"

If you prefer, however, you can go more slowly and add centers over several months as needed for variety and to support differentiated instruction. You might find it works better to add just four or five more centers so the students have three choices each day. The Word Center takes the place of the ABC Center now, because the letter recognition and sound work are moving to the whole-word level. But you can keep both if needed—it all depends on this year's class, doesn't it?

WEEK 10 Word Center

MATERIALS AND DIRECTIONS TO START YOUR WORD CENTER

- Rainbow Writing (see page 41)
- Mix-It, Fix-It (see page 43)

MATERIALS TO ADD LATER

- Plastic eggs with word families

  - Buy plastic eggs in the spring and use thick permanent marker.

  - On the longer part of the egg, write a word family chunk in permanent ink (example: *-op, -ug, -ail*).

  - On the short rounded part, write consonants, blends and digraphs (example: *c, th, sn*).

  - Differentiate this center by giving groups eggs that have the pattern you want to review. Students record words in My Word books.

- Sliders to practice word families with beginning consonants and blends

  - Write consonants on strips of colored tag board that are taped together.

  - Write blends and digraphs on another color of tag board that makes a strip that is taped together.

  - Make small cards of some of the most common rimes to slide down the strip to make word-family words (see photo in blue frame).

- Magnetic Wall: Make it a Word Center after using it as an ABC Center. (See page 23 for details on magnetic wall paint.) Use your magnetic letters and attach strip magnets to pictures or buy materials from Scholastic's Little Red Tool Box.

Morgan rotates the parts of each egg to create word family words like *stop, flop*, etc.

Le'Nell slides the red word chunk down the blue strip with blends and digraphs to create words.

- ◎ Word tubs
  Purchase small plastic tubs with lids or save margarine containers.

  - In each tub, put five small word cards with high-frequency words to review from the word wall.

  - Add the magnetic letters needed to make those five words.

  - Students build the words to match the cards and then record them.

Picture magnets can be used to match to beginning letters or build simple words.

Specific Mini-Lessons for the Word Center

- ◎ Make and post a chart that describes what the center will look like and sound like.

- ◎ As I introduce new activities, I do mini-lessons demonstrating how to use the materials and record the work.

Observation Center

MATERIALS

- ◎ Observation journals (small notebooks for writing observations in science and social studies throughout the year); you can have a class journal for each topic or students can record in their own journal that is used for recording all center work

- ◎ Magnifying glasses

- ◎ Date stamp to date entries

- ◎ Children's treasures: shells, leaves, rocks, pinecones, and so on

- ◎ Living creatures: ant farm, polliwogs, silkworms, butterflies, ladybugs

- ◎ Class pets: rat, hamster, guinea pig, goldfish, hermit crab

Tiny word tubs hold letters and word cards to practice spelling independently.

Specific Mini-Lessons for the Observation Center

- ◎ Make and post a chart that describes what the center will look like and sound like.

- ◎ Brainstorm words to use pertaining to each new item in the center. These words will be on a small stand-up chart that stays in the center.

- ◎ Write observations and make a simple picture.

- ◎ Write scientific questions: I wonder? Why? What if?

I record words the class uses to describe our silkworms that are in our observation area by the sink.

Overhead Projector

After building words with magnetic letters on the overhead, Morgan records the words in her center journal.

MATERIALS

- Overhead Projector
- Screen or wall to project images
- Poems on transparencies that have been laminated or are in sheet protectors
- Stories on transparencies that have been laminated or are in sheet protectors
- Wet-erase pens
- Baby wipes or other moist towels for cleanup
- Magnetic letters for letter sorting or word making with high-frequency words

Specific Mini-Lessons for the Overhead Projector Center

- Make and post a chart that describes what the center will look like and sound like.
- Model and practice how to adjust the top of the projector so that it shows only on the bottom of the screen (so that the work doesn't distract others).
- Model and practice building words from the word wall. Record in My Word Book.
- Model and practice reading the poems and stories and circling word wall words.
- Model and practice cleaning up the transparencies (or train an upper-grade helper to do the cleanup for you later).

Reading the Room

MATERIALS

- "Kid-level" print posted around the classroom (The modeled writing that is done after Mystery Name every day is posted low and provides a good beginning.)
- Pointers (fancy ones can be bought or use inexpensive dowels and yardsticks)
- Frames from old glasses (Optometrists will often donate outdated samples.)
- Children's inexpensive sunglasses with the lenses out
- Jumbo-size (2½-gallon) zippered bag to hold all material with plastic skirt hanger

Preston reads around the room with first-grade-style glasses.

Specific Mini-Lessons for Reading the Room

- Make and post a chart that describes what the center will look like and sound like.
- Model finding and reading all print around the room on walls, windows, doors, calendar, and charts.
- Review proper and improper use of pointers.
- Model quiet reading so we don't disturb others.

MATERIALS

- Poems we have practiced thoroughly in the Pocket Chart Center
- Gallon-size and snack-size zippered bags to store individual poems
- Laminator or plastic sleeve protectors
- Large roll of 2" clear packaging tape
- Jumbo-size zippered bag to hold all the poems.

Prepare Materials for Your Center

Make three copies of the poem on colored cardstock.

1ST COPY

- Trim outside edges to fit a gallon-size zippered bag.
- Laminate or put in plastic sleeve protector.
- Tape to outside bag using packaging tape. You now have a permanent storage bag for this poem

2ND COPY:

- Cut into sentence strips.
- Store inside the gallon-size zippered bag above.

3RD COPY

- Cut into individual words.
- Place words in a snack-size zippered bag and store inside the gallon-size bag.

TIP!

Use a different-color cardstock to copy each poem you use during the school year, so that small poem pieces are easily returned to their large zippered bag.

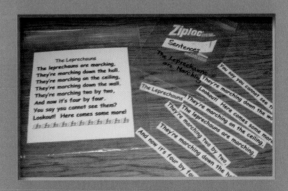

The Leprechauns
The leprechauns are marching,
They're marching down the hall.
They're marching on the ceiling,
They're marching down the wall.
They're marching two by two,
And now it's four by four.
You say you cannot see them?
Lookout! Here comes some more!

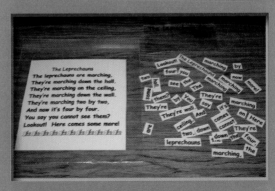

Specific Mini-Lessons for Poetry Center

- Make and post a chart that describes what the center will look like and sound like.
- Model and practice choosing a poem and cleaning up when finished.
- Match poem with the sentence strips.
- Mix it, rebuild sentence strips without matching (turn it over, check when done).
- Match words.
- Mix it, rebuild without matching (turn it over, check when done).
- Copy poem into center journal.

Center Management

By the third month of school, there are 12 centers up and running. Each day a group has three choices and students can go to them in any order. Because they can start at any of their choices for the day, the first graders are spread out, and there are usually no more than two or three students at any one center.

If You Want Everyone to Go to a Center

If you have a center that you want everyone to use, put the icon for that center in the chart for every day. The icon is a reminder, but the expectation is set that it is a "Must do." For example, I want every student to go to the Book Tub Center, so I put it in every groups' rotation.

Your chart might look something like the one in the photo below:

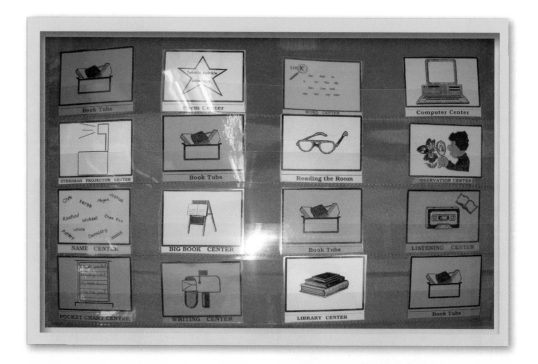

Optional Centers for Variety

Writing the Room

MATERIALS

- Small clipboards and 5" x 8" index cards (see page 21)
- Pencils

Specific Mini-Lessons for Writing the Room Center

- Make and post a chart that describes what the center will look like and sound like.
- Model and practice writing words from all around the room: word wall words, calendar notations, labels, and so on.

Print at first-grade eye level provides many words to write.

Travel Agency

MATERIALS

- Brochures from travel locations and sightseeing destinations (Brochures are available near the check-in desk of any local hotel.)
- Travel catalogues from travel agencies
- First-Grade Travel Agency form

Specific Mini-Lessons for Travel Agency Center

- Make and post a chart that describes what the center will look like and sound like.
- Brainstorm places we would like to go.
- Look at brochures and catalogs for what we will see, opening times, and cost.
- Model filling out the First-Grade Travel Agency form (see example at right).

First-Grade Travel Agency
Trip Planner

Where?_____

When will you go?_____

How will you get there?
☐ Car ☐ Plane ☐ Train ☐ Ship

What will you see?_____
_____
_____

Hours Open _____

What does it cost? $_____

Who will go with you? _____
_____
_____

TIP!

The Travel Agency is a great center to add before spring vacation.

Planning a trip involves practice answering questions: Where? When? How? What? Who?

Retraining as Needed to Maintain Centers and Sanity

Do your first graders "forget" what to do at centers, how to clean up, or how to work quietly so that reading groups aren't disturbed? Mine too! I call this "first-grade amnesia." I have trained them thoroughly, but they were "certified" months back or perhaps there are new students who aren't ready to be independent. So, I retrain as necessary. Here is a photo of the Book Tub Center in February. The center is a mess! Whenever these problems come up, I take the time to retrain and go over the procedures on the "What will we see?" "What will we hear?" charts.

Old Centers With a New Twist

I always start with the most basic activities and materials in each of our centers. First graders don't need to be dazzled and distracted with too many choices. After centers are established, I add more materials that are seasonal, topical with units of study, or that provide better differentiation. Here are some examples of activities Carolyn and I added throughout the year to our Writing Center:

Writing Center: Written Conversation

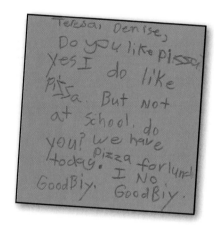

MATERIALS

- clipboard with plain paper
- pencils
- topic list for writing ideas

DIRECTIONS BEFORE WRITING

- Explain that students can now write a note with a partner when visiting the Writing Center.
- Instead of talking, they can take turns writing their words down on the clipboard paper.
- Brainstorm possible topics on a small chart.
- Model choosing a partner and a topic to write about with very quiet "private" voices.
- Make and post a chart that describes what the center will look like and sound like.

DIRECTIONS DURING WRITING

- Both partners put their names at the top of the paper on the clipboard.
- First student writes a question and passes the clipboard quietly to the partner.
- Second student reads the question then writes an answer and a new question.
- The clipboard is passed back and forth as the partners have a written conversation.

TOPICS
- Your weekend
- Your family
- Your pets
- Sports
- Toys
- Vacations
- Books
- Food
- Animals
- School

Writing to Family

MATERIALS

⦾ Index cards for postcards

⦾ Paper of various sizes

⦾ Envelopes (Parents can donate or pick up free stationery on hotel stays.)

SPECIFIC DIRECTIONS

⦾ Brainstorm family vocabulary on a small chart.

⦾ Make a model of a letter to post by the chart.

FAMILY
- Mom
- Dad
- brother
- sister
- aunt and uncle
- granma
- grandpa
- cousin

Dear _____,

Love,

_____

Everybody practices writing letters to family for a week.

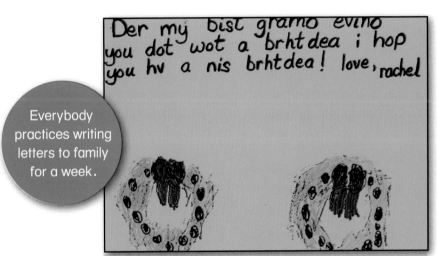

"Dear My Best Grandma, Even though you don't want a birthday I hope you have a nice birthday" Love, Rachel

Dear Shannan I wood
Love you to BayB
Sit Me Miss
Linch is mr teechn

Meridith decided to expand her writing to include my daughter Shannon—offering her a baby sitting job!

"Dear Shannon, I would love you to baby sit me. Mrs. Lynch is my teacher"

Question Kids

First-grade teacher and friend Betsy Stenklyft gave me this idea and the staff at your school will love it.

MATERIALS

- Paper, pencils and chart of school personnel
- Model letter posted at writing center

SPECIFIC DIRECTIONS

- Brainstorm school staff members on a small chart (we used their actual names).
- Brainstorm question words and sample questions.

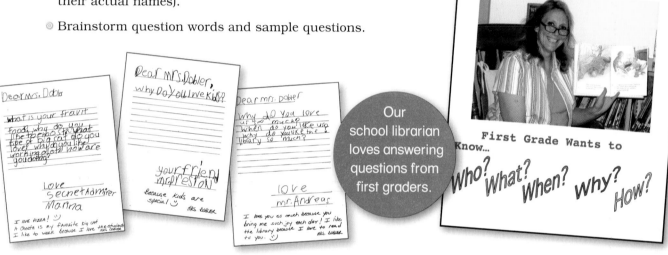

Our school librarian loves answering questions from first graders.

Writing Compliments

These letters can be bound into a class book to be read in class and taken home to be shared nightly with parents.

MATERIALS

We again use the cans and sticks labeled with student names that served us at the beginning of the year.

- Paper
- Tongue depressors with each student's name
- Cans labeled "1" and "2"

SPECIFIC DIRECTIONS

- Choose a tongue depressor from the first can to select the person who will get a compliment.
- Write that person a letter, put it in the class mail box and put his or her name in the second can.
- Choose another child's name from the first can and write another complimentary letter. Be sure to send a letter to each child.

I Can Read:

Our "I Can Read" board grows throughout the year with words students can read.

Reading Throughout the Year

Reading in first grade includes read-alouds, shared reading with Big Books and poetry, guided reading in small groups with leveled texts, and independent reading. I also use a standards-based basal for whole-class instruction. Each of these helps me have a balanced reading program and "drench" first graders in literacy.

Read-Alouds

I like to choose from a variety of chapter books, picture books, and nonfiction books to read aloud each day.

Chapter Books

There should be time each day when we immerse children in an ongoing story with few illustrations.

I tell them that watching television and playing video games cheats their imagination because all the pictures are created for them. A chapter book lets them form the images from the rich language they hear. I sometimes stop and say, "What do you see?" I like to read classics like *Winnie the Pooh* to start because each chapter is a self-contained story. Soon, children are ready for my all-time favorite, *Charlotte's Web.* Many years ago I got a note from a former student, Ian, when he was in fifth grade. At home his mother was reading his little sister *Charlotte's Web* and it reminded him of when he first heard the story in my class. Yes, to this day I cry when Charlotte dies and first graders have been known to say, "Get her the tissues again."

In the spring we study butterflies, ladybugs, silkworms, and tadpoles. At the same time that these creatures fill our classroom with wonder, it is time to read Roald Dahl's *James and the Giant Peach.* Every chapter has a cliffhanger—perfect for predicting what will happen next. I skip a couple of inappropriate words in the book, but the rest of the language is engaging and hilarious.

Every year I read *Charlotte's Web* and we learn about friendship.

My mom is reading Ashley Charlotte's Web. I remember you reading it to us in first grade with the book in one hand and a tissue in the other.

Love,
Ian

A former first grader writes to me.

Creatures fill the classroom in spring with topics to read and write about.

FAVORITE FIRST-GRADE CHAPTER BOOKS AND LONGER STORIES

- **Winnie the Pooh**
  by A.A. Milne

- **Mercy Watson Series**
  by Kate Di Camillo

- **Nate the Great Series**
  by Marjorie Weinman Sharmat

- **Magic Tree House Series**
  by Mary Pope Osborne

- **The Littles Series**
  by John Peterson

- **Matilda**
  by Roald Dahl

- **Magic School Bus Series**
  by Joanna Cole and Bruce Degen

- **Flat Stanley Series**
  by Jeff Brown

- **Charlotte's Web**
  by E. B. White

- **James and the Giant Peach**
  by Roald Dahl

- **Frog and Toad series**
  by Arnold Lobel

- **My Father's Dragon Series**
  by Ruth Stiles Gannett

Beginning Chapter Books and Informational Texts

I choose fiction that features powerful themes and favorite authors and characters. Kids love Clifford, Franklin, Arthur, Miss Nelson, and that naughty Junie B. Jones. I also want kids to get hooked on series that they will be able to read at the end of first grade and into second and third grades.

Nonfiction is the foundation of my teaching in science and social studies. I teach both thematically and interweave informational texts as a springboard for writing about what we have learned. How else can we find time to teach the content areas when our daily focus is on reading, writing, and math? Before starting each unit of study I do a first-grade version of the Ogles's (1986) KWL (what they know, what they want to know or will learn, and what they have learned). First graders don't have the depth of knowledge to claim "I know...," so we are more tentative and start with "I think." Here is what our chart will come to look like over time:

I think...	*I wonder...*	*I learned...*
Brainstorm what students **think** they know about the new topic. Accept all answers.	Write **"I wonder"** questions so students have reasons to research the topic.	When done, write everything students have **learned.**

Shared Reading With Poetry Throughout First Grade

Teaching with poetry is so effective with first graders because our instruction can include all the components that support learning to read. A poem in the pocket chart lends itself to repeated readings as we work with it every morning for a week or two. Students will do shared reading as we read each poem with gusto and pizzazz. Rhyme, rhythm, and repetition are all supports for emergent readers.

Poems become longer and more complex as we move through the year.

Poetry is a natural at helping students with phonemic awareness—the ability to hear the sounds in language—because it tunes students in to hearing sounds and rhymes. Reading poetry also supports phonics instruction, which can be systematic even in this context, moving from lines of poetry, to individual words, to letters. As the year progresses, I choose longer and more complex poems, further developing students' phonics skills in a systematic way. Yes, I am explicit about letters and words and sounds in poetry—as I think out loud about how each works, students are gaining valuable information about our language.

Poetry work in the pocket chart supplements and supports all the other phonics instruction we do in first grade, but it is definitely the most fun. Also important for first-grade teachers: poetry is cheap! Put your favorite poem on sentence strips in your pocket chart and you are good to go. Make an extra set for matching and cutting up into word cards and letters and you are set to teach phonics.

Whole-class poetry work starts our day.

Whole-Class Poetry Work

At the beginning of first grade I use the "How Do You Do?" poem that I copied off the wall of a first-grade teacher's class in Auckland, New Zealand, more than 20 years ago. I love its simplicity, the chance to feature student names, and the introduction to high-frequency words (*how, do, you, my, are, who*). I do "Mystery Name" every morning the first four to five weeks of school (see page 33).

As the year progresses, students are ready for more challenging texts, so the poems I choose need to be more complex. I follow Terry Johnson's work in *Literacy Through Literature* (1987) to guide my poetry selections. Here is how I use my first-grade version of "Take Me Out to the Ball Game" in the spring of first grade.

Take me out to my little league game,

Take me out with my friends.

Buy me some nachos and soda pop,

I don't care if it ever ends.

With a cheer, cheer, cheer for my team,

If they don't win it's a shame.

For it's 1,2,3 strikes you're out,

At the old ball game.

Whole-Group Work

I introduce the poem and talk about its content to build background knowledge. For English learners, the class acts out the poem and plays a practice game of baseball with a wiffle ball for P.E.

We work with this poem/song a little bit each day for about two weeks. We sit on the rug by the calendar during the morning opening, with the poem displayed on the pocket chart, and do one of the following activities.

Tips for Repeated Reading

I read a line and students echo back.

Boys read a line and then girls do.

The right side of the room reads a line, and then the left side.

Alternate rows on the rug read a line.

Read it with a whisper.

Read it like a ghost.

Repeated Readings for Shared Reading: I read the poem to students and then they start chiming in. Next, I read it with them or have students come up to be "Teacher" while pointing under each word, using different ways to read it together as the days go by (see above).

Le'Nell loves to be "teacher" and point while the class reads along.

Matching: I number the lines in the poem on the pocket chart, and I print each line on a sentence strip. I show students a sentence strip and ask them which line in the poem it matches. To ensure everyone participates, I have children show with their fingers the number of the line the sentence strip matches. So if I show "Take me out with my friends," students hold up two fingers.

To increase the level of challenge, I have students match words and letters to the line in which they occur in the poem. Sometimes we even match word wall words. I invite a student who has located the word or letter to come up to the pocket chart and point to it with the pocket chart highlighter.

Scrambling the Poem; Rebuilding Without Matching: After matching becomes easy, I start scrambling up the poem's lines and eventually the words too. Without the poem to match, the students must hold the words in memory AND read them. This is a huge game for first graders, who must close their eyes and cover them while I mix up the poem. When I give the signal to open their eyes, a rug full of students are intently reading and reading the poem, looking for the mismatch. They think this is a blast while I just smile at all the reading practice they are getting.

Early in the year, I usually just scramble lines of the poem. But as the year progresses I cut the lines into words and increase the challenge. You can take a very simple poem and make it challenging by cutting it into words and then mixing them up. No longer is reading this poem "mindless memorizing"—they are doing the reading work needed to rebuild it.

A blue pocket chart highlighter is used to find the word wall word *with*.

Small-Group Work With Poetry

I often make individual copies of a poem for a reading group. Sometimes I do this to provide further practice with the poem in the pocket chart for a group that needs more scaffolding to read it successfully. Or, I may pick a more challenging poem for the reading group that needs differentiation. One of my favorite sources for poems is the *Random House Book of Poetry* by Jack Prelutsky (1983). The indexes in the back include an Author Index, Title Index, First Line Index, and Subject Index. I use the Subject Index to choose poems that supplement the science and social studies thematic studies or seasonal topics. Here's how to use poetry instead of books with a small group over the course of several days:

DIRECTIONS

1. Make two copies of the poem for each student.

2. Discuss the topic of the poem and front-load key vocabulary into your discussions.

3. Invite students one at a time to read and reread from their personal copy while you listen and coach reading strategies.

4. Use the second copy of the poem to match sentences.

   ◎ Cut into sentence strips.

   ◎ Scramble the sentences.

   ◎ Have students match the sentence strips on top of their personal copy and then read and reread it carefully.

   ◎ Have students turn the personal copy over and rescramble the sentences.

   ◎ Have students rebuild the poem on the table, then read and reread it carefully.

   ◎ Have students turn the personal copy over and check their work.

5. On another day, use the cut-up poem to match words.

   ◎ Cut the sentence strips into individual words.

   ◎ Scramble the words.

   ◎ Have students match the words on top of their personal copy, then read and reread it carefully.

   ◎ Have students turn the personal copy over and rescramble the words.

   ◎ Have students rebuild the poem on the table. Read and reread carefully.

   ◎ Have students turn the personal copy over and check their work.

Poetry Center

Poems for this center come from the ones used in previous weeks in the Pocket Chart Center or from small-group work described above. Students can now work independently during guided reading on poems that are added throughout the year.

Guided Reading Throughout the Year

Guided reading evolves and changes throughout the year. Everything from the strategy focus in lessons to the makeup of groups to the books you choose and the reading level of students—nothing stays the same in first grade.

No matter what the text level, I incorporate Marie Clay's coaching for reading cues when listening to individuals read. I prompt for:

1. Meaning and comprehension by asking, ***"Does that make sense?"***

2. Structure/using syntax and grammar by asking, ***"Does that sound right?***

3. Visual information/phonics by asking, ***"Does that look right?"***

Are they frozen at an unknown word or are they looking at print in more complex ways? I model and teach for each of these strategies:

- Look across the word to use all the letters for information.

- Ask "What do I know" to find any part of the unknown word that is known.

- Chunk the word to use common patterns to break a word into larger parts.

- Look into the word for complex vowel patterns and multiple syllables.

- Ask "What other sound can I try?" when a word is mispronounced and doesn't make sense.

I supplement our book reading with an occasional strategy or skill lesson focusing on what students need. For example, if a group needs to practice "Look across the word," we can do a word sort that encourages them to do just that.

A word sort reinforces the strategy "Look across the word."

If a reading group is ready to start chunking words, I do lessons that show them the common patterns. In the photo to the right, we've paused at the end of our guided reading group to brainstorm a pattern that was in the book we just finished: *ay*.

These lessons follow students' reading needs carefully and guarantee differentiation.

Changing Groups

Ongoing informal teacher assessment and occasional running records help us determine the makeup of reading groups throughout the year. Informally, day after day, I am looking for children's use of the cueing systems above and

Looking for the chunk *ay*. We found it in our book and in TayBrieja's name.

reading strategies such as monitoring (noticing if there is something wrong with their reading), cross-checking (using more than one source of information, such as checking the picture and the print), rereading to get more information, and self-correcting.

In the picture to right, I'm doing a quick running record with one student while the rest of the group warms up by reading yesterday's book, *The Doorbell Rang*. Notice the rest of the group is using reading phones so their voices are very low.

I do a quick running record with Carlos while the rest of the group warms up by rereading yesterday's book.

I change groups based on running records and my daily observations. How is each first grader using meaning, structure, and phonics cues to decode a new text? If I move a student into a higher or lower group, I "double dose" him or her for a couple of weeks. This means the student stays in the original group *and* goes to the new one. This transition time helps me assess how the student is doing in the new group and builds his or her confidence. I also talk to the child's parents and send extra books home to help with the change.

Choosing Books

When first graders begin using a strategy, I move them into the next level of text. As I mentioned earlier, leveled readers will increasingly have larger amounts of print on a page, less support from the pictures, less scaffolding with repetitions, and more complex language structures and content. I spend one to three weeks on a level, so that students will read between five and fifteen books as needed before moving on.

I train parents to look at the number of words on a page, picture support, and complexity as they choose books for their child. My goal is that parents can support their first-grade reader when checking books out from the library or choosing books at a store or book fair. Informed parents strengthen our reading program.

I train parents to pick "just-right" books for their beginning readers.

Independent Reading

There are several main sources of independent reading materials in my first-grade classroom.

Book Baskets by Author/Series or Topics of Interest

Baskets of these books are sorted by favorite series or authors such as Clifford, Franklin, Curious George, Dr. Seuss, and so on. Topics of interest include bears, colors, numbers, ABCs, friends, dinosaurs, frogs, butterflies, and holidays. The front of each basket has a label with a picture of the cover of the main book in the series or on the topic. To get this picture, I can scan the book cover or copy the picture of the cover from an online book source. I copy the small online picture, paste it into a word document, size the book cover picture to about 3" x 4", copy in color and attach this tag to the end of the basket on rings. The tag on the basket makes it easy for first graders to return the book to the basket.

Tim listens to Jack read after lunch. He is one of the Book Buddies who come in every day.

The readability of these books tends to be in the higher two ranges. Some first graders will honestly only "browse" in these books for part of the year unless paired up with intermediate buddies. I have a couple of Book Buddies come in after lunch each day. They give up their own recess to read with first graders and build their "reading mileage."

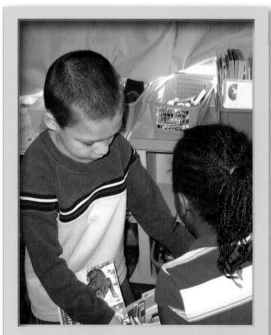

Trevor and Lexus take down a book basket to read from.

Classroom Library

A shelf of books that don't fit into a collection above are always available. The readability of these literature books tends to be in the higher two ranges. I can't count on these books for true independent practice, which is supposed to be in the 95-100% accuracy range (only 1 error in 20 words).

Book Baskets From Guided Reading

This is a powerful source for independent reading because the books are leveled texts already read in reading groups. The books read in guided reading are kept in this basket for about two weeks before returning them to the book room. I expect familiar reading out of this basket one to two times a day.

Class Books Rewritten From Old Favorites

Especially at the beginning of the year, I create class books that are rewritten in the pattern of old favorites. The first class book will have an individual page for each first grader from the poem "How Do You Do?" (see page 32). Early in the year we will also make our own version of *Brown Bear, Brown Bear* by Bill Martin, Jr., and Eric Carle. Kids love the repetitive pattern even more when their own pictures are in the class book. I keep a tub of these books for independent reading, and it fills up throughout the year.

Timmy, Timmy What do you see?

I see Devin Looking at me.

Take-Home Book Checkout—Keep it Simple!

Dear Families,

I am going to start sending books home for you child to read with you each night. It is very hard for parents to find books for first graders to read close to their level---so I will provide them! The books will be in a range close to what your child reads. Some will seem easy and others will be a challenge. Please read the book together first and then have your child read to you.

The books will come home Monday through Thursday nights. Your child will have a zip lock bag with his or her name on it. Please get in a routine each day of reading together, putting the book back in the bag and putting it in your child's backpack. If you lose a book, please send $5.00 as a deposit until it is found. I really want the books and not the money! My goal is that you and your child enjoy reading.

P.S. If you have books you would like to donate, please let me know.

I notify parents when the take-home book program will begin at back-to-school night and with a letter.

Now, in the real world, of course some kids forget to bring their books back! I have a reminder paper that students fill out and take home that day. Still, I do lose some books. But parents know books are coming home every night Monday through Thursday, and usually the reminder works. If worse comes to worst, I ask families to pay $5 for the lost book. I put the money in an envelope with the child's name on it and the parents know they can get the money back if the book is ever found (under the couch, behind the dresser) before the last day of school. For students who can't afford the $5.00, I privately have them "work" for me to pay for the book. For first graders, this means sharpening pencils or straightening bookshelves during a few recesses. I'm committed to sending books home with students that are at their independent reading level to give them lots of extra practice. Parents, affluent or not, have little access to truly leveled materials.

Take-Home Bags

You can buy take-home book bags at teacher supply stores (call 1-800-ART-READ for a catalog), but they can be pricy. I stick with the zipped bags I can get at the grocery store and easily label for each child, using computer address labels. Each child's name is handwritten in the middle of the label, attached to the bag, and covered with 2-inch-wide clear packing tape for durability.

REMINDER . . .

needs to return:

Book Checkout Chart

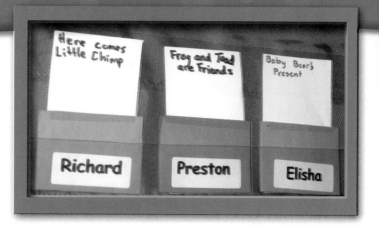

In the past, I made a chart on half of a large colored posterboard. I glued library pockets with each child's name on the board and attached the board to a door or cupboard. This year I tried something new. I bought a thin, vertical hanging pocket chart and hung it on the side of the four-sided rack. This rack holds a pocket chart on each side and has a shelf at the bottom. I am trying the pocket chart this year because it saves making the chart each year on posterboard. I just put a colored name tag for each child and students can put the book's title card behind their name. When I found the name cards were slipping around, I secured them with some tape. Another good checkout system is a shoe holder that hangs over a door and has plastic pockets—a perfect place for each student to put the 3" x 5" index card from the book he or she is taking home that night.

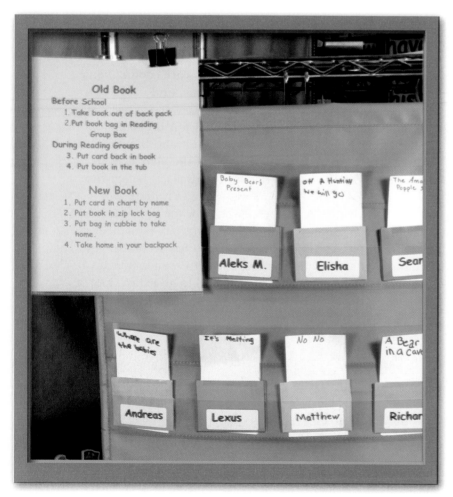

Checkout Procedures

I attach a copy of the book checkout directions above the pocket chart with student names.

I model and students practice following these steps for several days before I actually send books home. When students take home a book from the tub, they take out the title card from inside the book and put it in the Take-Home Book Checkout by their name. When they bring the book back the next morning, they put their book bag in their reading group's book box. During guided reading, they return the book. They have to remember to put the title card back inside the book, return it to the correct tub, and choose another. I can glance at the chart and see who has which book.

Old Book

BEFORE SCHOOL

1. Take book out of backpack. Sometimes children ask to read their book to the teacher when they get it out of their book bag. If school hasn't started yet, there is often time to listen to a few read on the rug. Others can read to a partner until the bell rings.

2. Put book bag in reading group box. Students are reminded to unload their backpacks each morning. They put their take-home book bag in the reading group box on the shelf under the window. Getting the book bags out of the backpack first thing each morning and in a place that is handy for use during guided reading organizes the first graders.

Jack and Nhu An choose a new book to take home.

DURING READING GROUPS

3. Put card back in book.

4. Put book in the tub.

Choose a New Book

1. Put card in chart by name.

2. Put book in zippered book bag.

3. Put bag in cubby to take home.

4. Take the book bag home in your backpack.

Trevor puts his new take-home book in his cubby to go home tonight.

Trevor checks out a new book by putting the card behind his name.

Word Walls Throughout the Year

I set the routines for word wall practice during the first five weeks of school, and I continue with those procedures throughout first grade. What will change are the complexity of the words and the increasing expectation that the word wall will be used as a reading and writing resource.

Continued assessment is vital to know whether each first grader is becoming proficient at reading and writing the high-frequency words needed. Informal assessment is done when practicing at the big word wall, and formal assessments are done on each student four times a year.

New words for the week are featured in a small pocket chart.

Practice reading the word wall words is snappy and fun.

Spice Up Routines

Memory Match

The Memory Match routines stay the same, but I build from four words in the early weeks (4 x 2 = 8 cards in the chart) to six words (6 x 2 = 12 words in the chart). I typically do five new words each week after the first five weeks. The extra two slots in Memory Match allow repeated review of a tricky word.

Memory Match expands to more words to review.

Partner Practice

I also add spice to word wall practice by doing partner work. Partners can practice using the new word in a sentence or testing each other when we say, "Close your eyes and spell the word to your partner."

Everyone gets a turn to talk with partner practice.

Maintaining First-Grade Writers' Workshop

The daily format of mini-lesson, student writing, teacher conferencing, and sharing in author's chair continues throughout the year. What changes is the focus on the craft and skills needed to meet standards. Writing evolves through developmental stages; I praise what children know and coach them on what they need next.

What First-Grade Writers Need to Know Next

- Writing needs to make sense.

- The conventions of print (spaces, capitals, punctuation, and spelling) and handwriting help the reader understand the message.

- Spelling has regular and irregular patterns.

- We can use common spelling patterns to spell words.

- We can use familiar words to spell new words (take a familiar word, *cat*, and use it to spell a new word, *splat*).

- Alphabet cards, wall charts, word walls, and simple dictionaries are helpful writing tools.

- To write a complete thought, we start it with a capital and end it with a period.

- Descriptive words (color, shape, size) make writing more enjoyable to read.

- We can expand on a topic to write four to six sentences to create a simple paragraph.

When we want to write descriptive words about a topic, we write the brainstormed words, like these about sea otters, on index cards. Then we put the words on a key ring—all the better if we find a key chain that matches the topic like the sea otter here. The words are then available to students wanting to write about the topic.

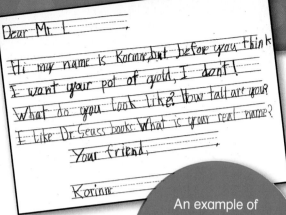

Dear Mr. L_____

Hi my name is Korinne, but before you think
I want your pot of gold, I don't!
What do you look like? How tall are you?
I like Dr. Seuss books. What is your real name?

Your friend,

Korinne

An example of question writing is this letter to a leprechaun that Korinne wrote (left) after the leprechaun visited our class.

Over time, we build a chart to encourage longer, more descriptive stories. Each one of these five on the list involved many mini-lessons over days and weeks. First graders need lots of modeling, examples, and conferencing on each point to "get it."

First Grade → Longer Stories
1. Details = tell more
2. Describe ⟨ size shape color 5 senses
3. Dialog = "talking"
4. Fiction = fake
5. Tell — Who? What? Where? When? Why?

Conferencing With First Graders

My goal is to conference with three to seven students each day. The length of time students write increases from 15 minutes in the fall to 35 minutes in the spring.

The lens a teacher uses when looking at writing:

- What do they know?
- What do they need?

These questions help me focus conferences.

I listen to the content of Preston's writing.

Here are examples of the same student on the first day of school, in October, and in February

Written on the first day of school, this string of capital letters is typical of early writing. He tells me it says "My Nintendo. I played my Nintendo. I played pro wrestling." *What does he know?* He knows that letters are written down to match speech, he goes from left to right, and he matches some letters to sounds (NT/Nintendo). *What does he need?* Everything! But I will focus on showing him how to say his words slowly and listen for sounds to write down. The ABC chart is close by as a resource.

NTI PPRMBSMKF

He reads his story to me when I lean in to hear, "I won the tigers ten to one," which is the first sentence in a four page story about his soccer game. *What does he know?* He knows high-frequency words (*the, to*), he is using the number chart to spell (*ten, one*), and he is hearing and recording more sounds in words (*wn/won, tigr/tiger*). *What does he need?* Spaces! Now he needs to be using a two-finger space between each spoken word. We say his sentence slowly and put each word on a finger—seven words to write, with spaces in between. I make a note on my clipboard that we worked on spaces, so I can follow up in the next few days.

I wn the tigr tento one

Yes, in February he is still writing about sports! That's okay because we encourage students to choose their own topics. *What does he know?* He can write for a sustained time on one topic. I asked him how he spelled *quarterback* and he took a quarter out of his pocket that was his milk money. He spells most words correctly and others phonetically. *What does he need?* At this point we want to add details, so we refer to the chart our class has been building over time: "Longer Stories."

I em a good football pleyr becus I mack a touchdown.
I wuos a quarterback
I passed to Ed he made a touchdown.

Closing Thoughts

It's June. The walls are bare and the furniture is again shoved into the corner so the classroom can be cleaned over the summer. Wait...isn't this what it looked like last August? I'm ready for summer...just like the kids! But it seems I always want a little bit more time with them. A few more guided reading lessons for the lowest reading group to solidify their reading strategies. A few more writing conferences to balance skills and the craft of writing. Are they ready for second grade, when it "really gets tough"? Have I done "enough"?

But I've done the best I can, and it is time to let them go. Give them a hug and send them on to second grade. And get ready to do it all again next year!

Computer Center 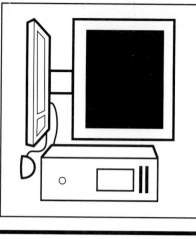	**Word Center** 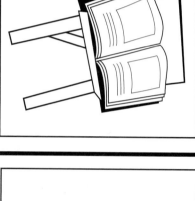
Observation Center 	**Big Book Center** 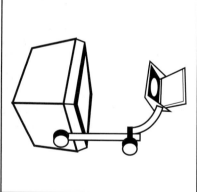
Reading the Room Center 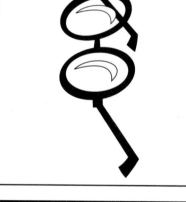	**Overhead Projector Center**
Poetry Center 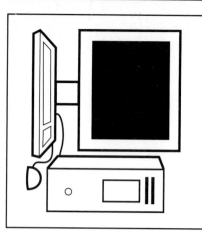 Twinkle, twinkle Little star...	**Pocket Chart Center** 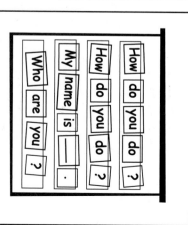